日本人英語初学者のための
基本動詞選定に関する研究

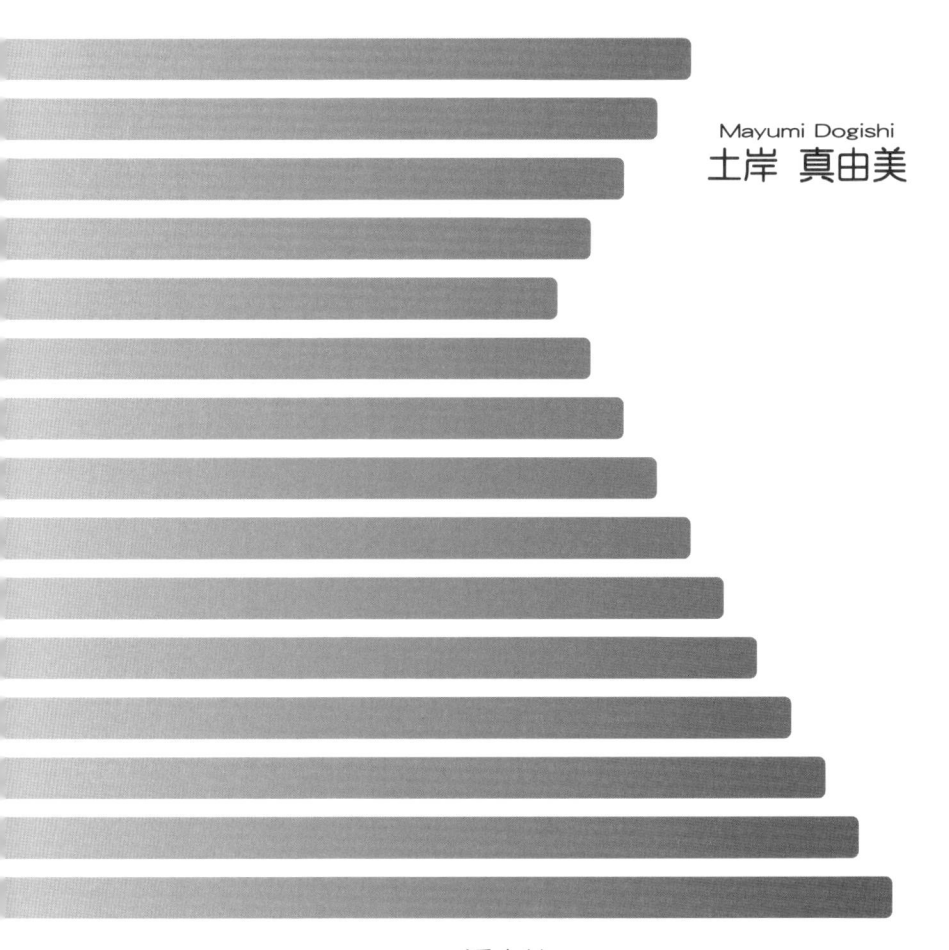

Mayumi Dogishi
土岸 真由美

溪水社

謝　　辞

　本書は，博士学位論文『日本人英語初学者のための基本動詞選定に関する研究』（安田女子大学大学院文学研究科2009年3月）に加筆・修正したものである。最終的に博士論文をまとめるに至る過程で，色々とご指導，ご助言を頂いた先生方に改めてお礼申し上げる。

　学部の卒論ゼミでは，安田女子大学の三宅英文先生にご指導頂いた。卒論では映画のスクリプトを用いて社会言語学的視点に基づく談話分析を行った。これが私の人生初の研究であり論文執筆であった。論文そのものは未熟なものであったが，三宅先生には社会言語学という研究領域の存在，論文の書き方や研究の難しさと楽しさを教えて頂いた。深く感謝申し上げる。

　大学院博士前期課程では英語学を専攻し，安田女子大学大学院の中川憲先生のもとで研究を行った。先生からは多くのことを教えて頂いたが，中でも英文の精読方法をしっかりとご教授頂いた。この時の文構造の理解の仕方はその後の中学校および高校で非常勤講師を務めるのに大変役立った。また修士論文のために扱った1,426語の新語を語形成の過程ごとに分類する作業は困難極まりなく，初めての英語での論文執筆には長い時間を要したが，それまでに味わったことのない達成感を感じることができたことは今でも私の大きな財産になっている。

　博士後期課程に進学するかどうかを迷っていた時，安田女子大学の松岡博信先生から「今度，僕の恩師の金田先生が山口大学を退官されて安田にいらっしゃるから，博士課程への進学を考えてみたら？」とアドバイスを頂いた。松岡先生のあの一言がなければ，今の私は存在していないだろう。松岡先生には学部生の頃から大学院を修了するまでの長い間，折に触れてお世話になった。記してお礼申し上げる。

大学院博士後期課程では金田道和先生のもとで英語教育学を学び，日本人英語初学者のための基本動詞選定を試みた。上述の通り，学部，博士前期課程，博士後期課程でそれぞれ異なる分野のテーマを選んで学んできた。最終段階で選ぶことになった英語教育学の領域は博士前期課程までの専門分野とは関連はあるものの，自分にとっては新しい専門知識や研究対象が多く，思うように英語教育学関連の論文がフォローできず，研究も行き詰まることも多かった。そのような時に金田先生からの「あんたはスタートが遅かったんだから気にするな」という一言で救われた気持ちになったことを思い出す。金田先生のもとで研究を続ける中で，先生の中立的で公平，かつ冷静な考え方や，学生への接し方，質問の仕方など，教育者としてだけでなく，人としても重要な多くのことを学ばせて頂いた。先生がいらっしゃらなかったら博士論文を書き上げ，本書を刊行することはできなかったと思う。

　また，安田女子大学の大槻和夫先生，広島大学大学院の深澤清治先生，県立広島大学の馬本 勉先生には，博士論文を完成するに当たり貴重なご助言を頂いた。

　博士前期課程，後期課程を通じて変わらず優しく見守ってくださった大学院事務室の土屋 文さん，そして多くの先輩，同輩，後輩の皆さんに支えられた実り多い学生時代であったことの幸せを今噛みしめている。皆さんにこの場を借りて謝意を表したい。

　大学院を修了し，幸いなことに教職に就くことができた今，私もいつかお世話になった先生方のような教師，そして研究者になりたいと切に思っている。

　そして私が何を研究しているかということは分からないと言いながらも，研究者への道を歩み始める大学院博士前期課程の学修を支援してくれた父と，いつでも背中を押して応援してくれる大きな存在であり続けてくれた母への感謝の思いは尽きない。長い間学生をさせて貰った分，これからは学んだことを社会に還元しながら，両親に誇りに思って貰えるような

娘を目指したい。

　最後になったが，本書の編集について温かく細やかなご助言をくださった溪水社の木村逸司氏にも記してお礼申し上げる。

　　　　　　　　　　　　　　　　　　　　　　　　土岸　真由美

は じ め に

　日本の英語教育において外国語として英語を学習する際，学習者が何を教材として何を学ぶかは，中学校学習指導要領（以下，学習指導要領と略す）に記載されている。しかし，平成10年に告示された学習指導要領には，学習すべき語彙数は900語とされているものの，語彙リストの記載が機能語を中心とする100語のみとなり，残りの約800語の選択は各教科書の任意によるものとなった。さらに平成20年告示の学習指導要領からは語彙リストの記載さえ無くなり，「1,200語程度」という教授する語の数のみが示されている。このことによって，教科書作成者は自由に語彙を選ぶことが可能となった。しかし，言語類型論的な面から見て，日本語と英語は全く対称的であると言われている。それゆえ何の根拠にも基づかず，バラエティー豊かなトピックに合わせただけの，使用場面が限られ，3年間で教科書に1，2度しか出てこないような語彙ばかりが選定されたのでは，学習者による英語構造の基本的な習得を期待することはできない。また，英語母語話者による使用頻度の高さを選定基準にして語彙を選定した過去の例はあるが，各語の持つ構造や特性までは考慮されていない。
　英語の学習は英語の構造の習得が第一である。そうでなければ，学習者が英語を「使える」ことにはならないからである。それゆえ英語の初期学習者に最初に提示すべき語彙は，英語の構造を学ぶために必要最低限の語彙でなければならないと考える。
　そのような語彙について共通の認識をするために，本書の第1章では，語を「知っている」と言うために必要な語彙に関する知識について，諸家の所説を概観した。そして語彙の学習が備えるべき特性と，その中でも日本人英語初学者が英語の基本構造を習得するための語彙学習が備えるべき特性を整理した。

第2章では，これまで外国人学習者のための英語の語彙リストを提案してきた動きが，外国人学習者のためのGraded readers（語彙制限をした読本）を求める動きの中にあったこと，また，それら歴史的語彙リスト（Basic English, *A General Service List of English Words*など）を考察し，現代において提案されている語彙リスト（竹蓋・中條，大学英語教育学会基本語リストなど）の共時的資料の特徴が「目標領域における語彙」を集積したものと捉え，その選定の基準が「語形の出現頻度」であることを確認した。

　さらに，英語母語話者によって実際に使用されている自然な英語の実態についても把握が必要であるため，第3章では，本書で基礎的データとして使用したThe British component of the International Corpus of English, *Longman Grammar of Spoken and Written English* (Biber, Johansson, Leech, Conrad, & Finegan, 1999), *Longman Lexicon of Contemporary English* (McArthur, 1981), それぞれの動詞の捉え方を基に基本動詞の持つべき特性をまとめた。

　また，日本の英語教育のこれまでの実態を把握するために，第4章では，外国語としての英語の教授と学習における語彙の扱いを，語彙リストを提示している過去の学習指導要領を用いてその変遷を考察し，40年余の時を経て常に「必修語」であり続けているものが80語あることを確認した。

　第5章では，英語母語話者が用いるclause typeの分布に基づいて，その相似形として，日本人英語初学者が学習すべき英語の動詞群を提案した。これに加えて，「意味」の観点から，英語母語話者が最も良く使う語義を語彙選定の基準の1つとし，さらに，外国語としての英語の学習という特殊な環境に必要な語彙を付加した。

目　次

謝　辞 ……………………………………………………………… i

はじめに …………………………………………………………… v

第1章　語を「知っている」とは：語の持つ情報 ………… 3
1.1　諸家の論 ……………………………………………… 3
1.2　語を「知っている」と言うために必要な知識 ……… 17

第2章　語彙リストの歴史的概観 ……………………………… 21
2.1　Basic English ………………………………………… 21
2.2　*A General Service List of English Words* ………… 23
2.3　「現代英語のキーワード」 …………………………… 25
2.4　『大学英語教育学会基本語リスト』 ………………… 26
2.5　The Longman Defining Vocabulary ………………… 28
2.6　まとめ ………………………………………………… 30

第3章　動詞の捉え方 …………………………………………… 33
3.1　The British component of the International Corpus of English ……………………………………… 33
3.2　*Longman Grammar of Spoken and Written English* ……… 58
3.3　*Longman Lexicon of Contemporary English* ……… 67

第4章　外国語としての英語の学習と語彙に関する調査 …… 73
4.1　調査資料 ……………………………………………… 73
4.2　調査対象 ……………………………………………… 74
4.2.1　必修語とその中の動詞の数および割合 ……… 74

  4.2.2 学習指導要領の動詞の clause type …………………………… 74

  4.2.3 学習指導要領の動詞の意味領域 ………………………………… 74

 4.3 調査結果 ………………………………………………………………… 75

  4.3.1 必修語とその中の動詞の数および割合 ……………………… 75

  4.3.2 学習指導要領の動詞の clause type …………………………… 76

  4.3.3 学習指導要領の動詞の意味領域 ………………………………… 79

 4.4 考察 ……………………………………………………………………… 81

  4.4.1 必修語とその中の動詞の数および割合について ………… 81

  4.4.2 学習指導要領の動詞の clause type について …………… 82

  4.4.3 学習指導要領の動詞の意味領域について ………………… 82

第5章 日本人英語初学者のための基本動詞リスト ……… 85

おわりに ……………………………………………………………………… 91

参考文献 ……………………………………………………………………… 95

付録 …………………………………………………………………………… 101

 付録1．ICE-GB の動詞 ………………………………………………… 101

 付録2．中学校学習指導要領の必修語として共通する動詞 ………… 154

 付録3．Fries and Fries（1961）の動詞 ……………………………… 155

 付録4．LDOCE の定義語内の動詞 …………………………………… 157

日本人英語初学者のための基本動詞選定に関する研究

第1章 語を「知っている」とは:語の持つ情報

　語を「知っている」という表現を耳にすることがあるが，多くの場合，その表現が意味するものは，今までにその語を「見たことがある」や，その語の持つ複数の語義のうちの「いくつかを知っている」というのが一般的である。例えば，学習者の語彙力を測るテストにおいて，どのような知識を測るのかを見れば，語を「知っている」と言うために，どのような知識を持っていることが要求されているのかが明らかとなる。本章では，まず，語を「知っている」と言うためにはどのような語彙知識を持っているべきかについて，複数の研究者の捉え方を概観する。そして，その中で日本人英語初学者が英語の語を「知っている」と言うために，語の持つ情報のうち，何をどこまで学ぶべきか，最低限必要な語彙についての知識を明らかにする。

1.1　諸家の論

　Nation (2001, p.27) は，語を「知っている」ことには受容語彙と発表語彙の別々の観点から，形(話し言葉，書き言葉，語の構成要素)，意味(語形と意味，概念と指示物，連想)，用法(文法的機能，コロケーション，用法における制約)を知っていることが含まれると述べている。

表1. *What is involved in knowing a word* (Nation, 2001, p.27)

Form	spoken	R	What does the word sound like?
		P	How is the word pronounced?

	written	R	What does the word look like?
		P	How is the word written and spelled?
	word parts	R	What parts are recognisable in this word?
		P	What word parts are needed to express the meaning?
Meaning	form and meaning	R	What meaning does this word form signal?
		P	What word form can be used to express this meaning?
	concept and referents	R	What is included in the concept?
		P	What items can the concept refer to?
	associations	R	What other words does this make us think of?
		P	What other words could we use instead of this one?
Use	grammatical functions	R	In what patterns does the word occur?
		P	In what patterns must we use this word?
	collocations	R	What words or types of words occur with this one?
		P	What words or types of words must we use with this one?
	constraints on use (register, frequency...)	R	Where, when, and how often would we expect to meet this word?
		P	Where, when, and how often can we use this word?

Note: R = receptive knowledge, P = productive knowledge

語のFormについて詳しく見ていくと，spoken formを知っていることには，その語を聞いた時に認識でき，意味を表すためにその語のspoken formを産出することができることが含まれている（Nation, 2001, p.40）。また，written formに関する知識としては，その語を目にした時に認識し，その語を綴ることができることが内包されている（Nation, p.44）。さらにword partsについては，その語が他の語にも見られる接辞と1つの語幹からできていることを知っていること，またその語のワード・ファミリーに

含まれる語を知っていることが含意されている（Nation, pp.46-47）。

次に語のMeaningに関する知識について学習者は，語形や意味を知っているだけではなく，その2つを関連付けることが必要だとされている（Nation, 2001, pp.47-48）。concept and referentsについては，英語の多義性について，1つの語の中に含まれる意味の範囲を見た場合，例えば*the bank of a river*や*the national bank*における*bank*のように，語源が異なるなどの理由から，語形は同じでも意味が大きく異なるもの（homonym）は異なる語として数えられ，学習されるべきだと述べられている（Nation, p.49）。ある特定の語が持つ複数の意味の中には，互いに明らかな関連を示すものもあるが，それらは同じ語として扱われるべきか，別な語として扱われるべきか検討すべき問題であるとされている。またNagyは，言語使用者が関連する意味を扱う方法は2つあり，その両方が普通の言語使用において重要であると指摘している：

1. The language user may have a permanent internal representation of each related meaning. This means that when the word form is met, the user has to select the appropriate sense of the word from those stored in the brain. This process can be called '**sense selection**'.
2. The language user has an underlying concept for a word that is appropriate for the range of meanings with which the word is used.... When the learner meets the word in use, the learner has to work out during the comprehension process what particular real world items the word is referring to. This process is called '**reference specification**'....
（Nagy, 1997 as cited in Nation, 2001, p.50）（太字は原文のまま）

複数の意味を持つ語の場合でも，その語が使用されている文脈によって最も適切な意味を選択できることや，ある語を見聞きした際に，その語が現実世界の何に言及しているのかを理解することが，語を「知っている」と

言うためには必要な知識である。しかし，全ての語義に共通して存在する概念を見ることで語を定義すれば，覚えなければならない語の数を減らすことができるとも述べられている（Nagy, 1997 as cited in Nation, 2001, p.51）。また，語のassociationsに関してMiller and Fellbaum（1991 as cited in Nation, 2001, p.52）は，メンタルレキシコンの中にある組織的構造を描写するためには，品詞ごとに区別することが重要だと述べている。最も普及力があり，重要な関係はsynonymyであるが，名詞，形容詞，動詞はそれぞれの品詞に適した意味上の関係を使っており，その品詞の独自の体系を持っていると述べられている。そして，Nation（p.55）は，synonymy, hyponymy, meronymy, antonymy, troponymy, entailmentという関係は，学習者が既に知っている語を使って整理し直すための有用な出発点になるだろうと主張している。

　語のUseに関する知識は，grammatical functionsとして，語を使うためにはその語の品詞は何か，またその語がどの文法パタンに当てはまるかを知っていることが必要だと述べられている（Nation, 2001, p.55）。さらにcollocationsの知識として，その語がどのような語と主に共起するかを知っていることが挙げられている（Nation, p.56）。また，連語はサイズ（一連の語の並びに含まれる単語の数），タイプ（内容語と機能語の連語［*look*と*at*］や，内容語と内容語の連語［*united*と*states*］），連語関係にある語の親密さ（*expressed* their own honest *opinion*），そして連語関係にある語の可能な範囲（*commit*と*murder, a crime, hara kiri, suicide*など）などが大きく異なっているため，このようなそれぞれについての詳細な情報も持っている必要があると述べられている（Nation, p.56）。最後にconstraints on useに関してNation（p.57）は，ほとんどの語は言語の社会的な面に関する要因によって使用を制限されてはいないが，言語の中には人について言及する際の言葉，特に話し手と言及されている人との関係を示す時に厳しい制限が加えられるものがあると述べている。確かに学習者は，そのことを予め知っておき，第2言語を使用する際に注意しておくべきだろう。

ここで，Nation (2001) に従って学習指導要領に必修語として挙げられた動詞のうち，The British component of the International Corpus of English の clause type (intransitive, copular, monotransitive, dimonotransitive, ditransitive, complex-transitive, transitive) のうちの6つ以上で使用可能であり，全ての clause type における出現頻度が10回以上である *get* を例として，この語の持つ情報を表2に整理してみる。発音記号に関しては The International Phonetic Association (1999) に準じて表記する。定義や用例は，*Longman Dictionary of Contemporary English* (Summers et al., 2003)（以下 LDOCE と略す）を使用し，concept and referents に関しては，田中他 (2003) の「コア」の概念を参照する。また，*get* の類義語に関しては *Webster's New Dictionary of Synonyms* (1984) を参照する。

表2．*get* という語を「知っている」と言うために持っているべき情報

Form	spoken	R	[gɛt]
		P	[gɛt]
	written	R	'get'
		P	'get'
	word parts	R	get
		P	get
Meaning	form and meaning	R	1 RECEIVE to receive something that someone gives you or sends you
			2 OBTAIN to obtain something by finding it, asking for it, or paying for it
			3 BRING to bring someone or something back from somewhere
			4 BUY a) to buy something b) to pay for something for someone else c) to buy a newspaper regularly
			5 MONEY a) to receive money for doing work b) to receive money when you sell

7

something
6 HAVE A FEELING/IDEA to start to have a feeling or an idea
7 HAVE/EXPERIENCE to have, do, or experience something
8 ILLNESS to catch an illness
9 ACHIEVE to achieve something
10 RECEIVE A PUNISHMENT to receive something as a punishment
11 ARRIVE to arrive somewhere
12 REACH A POINT to reach a particular point or stage of something
13 **get (sb) somewhere/anywhere/nowhere** if you get somewhere, or if an action gets you somewhere, you make progress
14 MOVE to move or go somewhere
15 MAKE STH MOVE to make something or someone move to a different place or position, especially with some difficulty
16 TRAVEL to travel somewhere on a train, bus etc
17 BECOME to change to a new feeling, situation, or state
18 MAKE SB/STH BECOME STH to make someone or something change to a new feeling, situation, or state
19 BE HURT/BROKEN ETC used to say that something, especially something bad, happens to someone or something
20 MAKE STH HAPPEN TO SB/STH a) to accidentally make someone or something experience something b) to do something, or arrange for it to be done

第1章　語を「知っている」とは：語の持つ情報

21 MAKE STH DO STH to make something do a particular thing
22 MAKE SB DO STH to persuade or force someone to do something
23 UNDERSTAND to understand something
24 COOK to prepare food or a meal
25 RADIO/TELEVISION to be able to receive a particular radio signal, television station etc
26 ANSWER THE DOOR/TELEPHONE to answer the door or telephone
27 CATCH SB to catch someone
28 HURT/KILL SB to attack, hurt, or kill someone
29 TRICK SB to deceive or trick someone
30 ON THE TELEPHONE if you get someone on the telephone, they answer the telephone when you have made a call, and so you talk to them
31 **get doing sth** to begin doing something
32 **get to do sth** to have the opportunity to do something
33 **get to like/know/understand sb/sth** to gradually begin to like, know, or understand someone or something
34 **you get sth** used to say that something happens or exists
35 **you've got me (there)** used to say you do not know the answer to something
36 **it/what gets me** used to say that something really annoys you
37 **get this** used to draw attention to something

9

				surprising or interesting that you are about to mention
		P	*get, gets, got, gotten, getting*	
	concept and referents	R	コア ある状態を得る	
		P	コア ある状態を得る	
	associations	R	synonym:	
			1 *get, obtain, procure, secure, acquire, gain, win*	
			2 *beget, procreate, sire, generate, engender, breed, propagate, reproduce*	
			3 *induce, persuade, prevail*	
		P	synonym:	
			1 *get, obtain, procure, secure, acquire, gain, win*	
			2 *beget, procreate, sire, generate, engender, breed, propagate, reproduce*	
			3 *induce, persuade, prevail*	
Use	grammatical functions	R	verb:	
			T not in passive (1, 8, 21, 22, 23, 24, 25)	
			T (2, 3, 4, 5, 6, 7, 9, 10, 16, 18, 19, 20, 26, 27, 28, 29, 30)	
			I always + adv/prep (11, 12, 14)	
			T always + adv/prep (15)	
			linking verb (17, 19)	
			T not in progressive (23, 25)	
		P	verb:	
			T not in passive (1, 8, 21, 22, 23, 24, 25)	
			T (2, 3, 4, 5, 6, 7, 9, 10, 16, 18, 19, 20, 26, 27, 28, 29, 30)	
			I always + adv/prep (11, 12, 14)	
			T always + adv/prep (15)	
			linking verb (17, 19)	
			T not in progressive (23, 25)	
	collocations	R	1 get sth from sb, get sth off sb	
			2 get sth for sb, get sb sth	

第1章　語を「知っている」とは：語の持つ情報

    3　get sb/sth from sth, get sth for sb, get sb sth
    4　a) get sth for sb, get sb sth, get yourself sth, get sth from sth, get sth for $20/£100/50p etc
    5　a) get £2000/$4000 etc for doing sth b) get £100/$200 etc for sth
    6　get pleasure from/out of sth
  17　get to be sth
  19　get hurt/broken/stolen etc, get sth caught/stuck etc
  21　get sth to do sth, get sth doing sth
  22　get sb to do sth, get sb doing sth
  23　get what/how/who etc
  24　get sb sth
  13, 31, 32, 33, 34, 35, 36, 37は"IDIOMS & PHRASES"

P 1　get sth from sb, get sth off sb
    2　get sth for sb, get sb sth
    3　get sb/sth from sth, get sth for sb, get sb sth
    4　a) get sth for sb, get sb sth, get yourself sth, get sth from sth, get sth for $20/£100/50p etc
    5　a) get £2000/$4000 etc for doing sth b) get £100/$200 etc for sth
    6　get pleasure from/out of sth
  17　get to be sth
  19　get hurt/broken/stolen etc, get sth caught/stuck etc
  21　get sth to do sth, get sth doing sth
  22　get sb to do sth, get sb doing sth
  23　get what/how/who etc
  24　get sb sth
  13, 31, 32, 33, 34, 35, 36, 37は"IDIOMS &

		PHRASES"
constraints on use (register, frequency…)	R	The word is one of the 1000 most common words in both spoken and written English; *spoken* (4b) *informal* (23, 26, 28, 29, 32); *especially AmE* (37); spoken phrases (34-37): それ以外に使用に関するラベル無し
	P	The word is one of the 1000 most common words in both spoken and written English; *spoken* (4b) *informal* (23, 26, 28, 29, 32); *especially AmE* (37); spoken phrases (34-37): それ以外に使用に関するラベル無し

　以上に見る通り，*get* についてこれらの情報を全て自らの知識とするならば，学習者は英語母語話者の持つ知識と変わらないものを持つことになるだろう。しかし，後述するように，これらの情報全てが，日本人英語初学者にとって必要であるとは考えない。

　「新しい語を学習するとは何か？」という問いに対し，Ellis（1997, p.123）は，最低限その新語を語として認識し，メンタルレキシコンに入れることだと述べている。さらにインプットとアウトプットで異なる4つの伝達経路のために特殊化した語の集合（lexicon）についても言及している。Ellis（p.123）によると発話を理解するには auditory input lexicon が新しい音のパタンを分類しなければならず，その語を読むためには visual input lexicon が新しい綴りのパタンを認識するようにならなければならない。また，その語を発するには speech output lexicon がその発音をするために運動プログラム（motor programme）を一致させなければならないし，その語を書くためには spelling output lexicon がその語の一連の綴りのための仕様書を持っていなければならない。さらに Ellis（p.123）は，我々は語の統語的特性を学ぶだけでなく，語彙構造におけるその語の位置（他の語との関連）や意味的特性，指示的特性，および伴立（命題と結論の関係）を

決定する際の役割，さらに概念システム全体におけるその語の位置を決める概念の基礎，そして意味的，概念的意味へのインプット／アウトプット仕様を結びつけることを学ばなければならないと述べている。

　Ellis（1997, p.123）は，上述した語彙習得の複数の異なる観点は，以下の2つの分離可能な学習メカニズムによって支えられていると論じている：

(i) the acquisition of a word's form, its I/O lexical specifications, its collocations, and its grammatical class information all result from predominantly unconscious (or implicit) processes of analysis of sequence information; (ii) the acquisition of a word's semantic and conceptual properties, and the mapping of word form labels onto meaning representations, results from conscious (or explicit) learning processes.

これらのメカニズムは英語母語話者に当てはまるものであるため，外国語として英語学習をする日本人英語学習者（特に初学者）には，「無意識の（あるいは暗示的な）」処理過程は当てはまらず，全ての英語の語彙知識を意識的（明示的）に学習する必要があることは当然である。いずれにせよ，上記の語彙知識がEllisの言う「新語を学ぶこと」に含まれる語彙知識である。これらをNation（2001）の挙げた9つの観点からの語の知識と比較し，その異同を見た結果は次の通りである。

　まずFormに関する知識の中のspoken formについては，Ellis（1997, p.123）にauditory input lexiconとspeech output lexiconへの言及があることから，前者がある語を聞いた時にその語であると認識し，後者がその語を正しく発音できることを意味していると考えられる。また，written formについてはvisual input lexiconと spelling output lexiconについての記述があることから（Ellis, p.123），前者がある語を目にした時にその語であると認識し，後者がその語を正しく綴ることができることを意味していること

13

がわかる。しかしながらEllis（1997）には，Nation（2001）のword partsに関する記述は見られない。

次にMeaningに関する知識であるが，form and meaningとしてEllis(1997, p.123)には語形を意味に結びつけることが言及されているため，Nation（2001）と同じ考え方であることが窺える。また，concept and referentsとして，Ellisには語の意味的特性と概念的特性への言及がなされている（p.123）。しかし，associationsについてはEllisでは言及されていない。

最後にUseに関する知識の中のgrammatical functionsについては，Ellis（1997, p.123）にも品詞の情報はあるが，Nation（2001）のように，その語が使用されるclause typeや文法パタンについての言及はなされていない。collocationsについてはEllis（p.123）も同じ用語を使用して触れている。しかし，constraints on useに関する言及はEllisには見られない。ここまでの結果から，語を「知っている」と言うために必要な語彙知識は，Nation（2001）に挙げられたものでカバーできると言うことができる。

Carter（1998, p.239）は，第2言語もしくは外国語の語を「知っている」と言うための7つの特性を次のように挙げている：

1 It means knowing how to *use* it productively and having the ability to *recall* it for active use, although for some purposes only passive knowledge is necessary and some words for some users are only ever known passively.（イタリックは原文のまま）

2 It means knowing the likelihood of encountering the word in either spoken or written contexts or in both.

3 It means knowing the syntactic frames into which the word can be slotted and the underlying forms and derivations which can be made from it.

4 It means knowing the relations it contracts with other words in the language and with related words in an L1 as well.

5 It means perceiving the relative coreness of the word as well as its more marked pragmatic and discoursal functions and its style-levels.
6 It means knowing the different meanings associated with it and, often in a connected way, the range of its collocational patterns.
7 It means knowing words as part of or wholly as fixed expressions conveniently memorized to repeat — and adapt — as the occasion arises.

上記の特性と Nation（2001）に挙げられた語を「知っている」と言うために必要な情報を重ね合わせて比較すると次のような結果となる。

まず Form に関する知識の中の，spoken form および written form について，Carter（1998, p.239）の1つ目に挙げられた特徴が当てはまる。しかし，word parts に関しては Carter の挙げる3番目の特徴の一部である「その語の基本形と派生形を知っていること」が含まれる。

次に Meaning に関する知識であるが，form and meaning に Carter（1998）の3番目の特徴の一部である「その語の基本形と派生形を知っていること」が相当し，また6番目の特徴の一部である「その語の持っている他の意味を知っていること」が当てはまる。そして concept and referents には Carter の挙げる5つ目の特徴のうち，「その語の相対的なコアネスを知っていること」が該当し，associations には Carter の4つ目の特徴が当てはまる。

最後に Use に関する知識の中の grammatical functions については，Carter（1998）の3つ目の特徴のうち「語が組み込まれうる統語構造を知っていること」が相当する。collocations については6番目の特徴のうち，コロケーションに関することが含まれている。constraints on use に関しては，Carter の挙げる2番目の特徴がその中の一部に該当し，また5番目の特徴のうち，「その語の表現形式レベルを知っていること」が当てはまる。Carter の挙げる7つ目の特徴は，Nation（2001）にも Ellis（1997）

にも挙げられていない，Carter独特の概念であると考えられる。LDOCE を用いて*get*を例にCarterの7つ目の特徴に当てはめる。以下はLDOCEに イディオムとして挙げられているものを全て挙げたものである。また，各 イディオムの前につけられた数字は，LDOCEの中の*get*の多義の出現頻度 順である：

    13　get (sb) somewhere/anywhere/nowhere
    31　get doing sth
    32　get to do sth
    33　get to like/know/understand sb/sth
    34　you get sth
    35　you've got me (there)
    36　it/what gets me
    37　get this

Carter（p.239）は7番目の特徴を「語を必要に応じて暗唱したり適当に変 えて転用したりするために，便利に覚えられる慣用表現の一部，もしくは 全面的なものとして知っていること」としている。

　Cook（2001, pp.60-61）によると，語彙を学習することは，意味を伴う長 い語のリストを習得することを意味している。以下にCook（pp.61-63）の 挙げる'man'という語の持つ側面について示す。

　語の形について言うと，我々はその語の発音を知っていなければならな い。例えば'man'の発音は/mæn/であるが，'chairman'のような複合語にお いては/mən/になることを知っていなければならない。また，語の形とし て綴りも知っていなければならない。語には特定の綴りがあり，その言語 の綴りのルールに基づいているのである。それゆえ，例えば'man'の中の 'n'は'-ing'が後続するときは重ねて綴られるということを知っていなけれ ばならない。

次に文法的特性に関しては，我々はその語の文法的範疇（品詞）と，その語が文構造においてどのような働きをするかを知っていなければならない。例えばその語が名詞であれば文の主語や目的語となる名詞句の一部となることや，動詞であれば動詞句の構成要素になることを知っている必要がある。そしてその語が使われる文構造も知っておく必要がある。例えば'man'が動詞であれば，その文は生物主語を持ち，目的語を取らなければならないことを知っていなければならない。言い換えると，これは動詞の'項構造（argument structure）'を知っておく必要があることになる。そしてその語の特異な文法的情報（例えば名詞の不規則変化した複数形の綴りや発音など，また可算名詞，不可算名詞の違いなど）も知っていなければならない。

さらに語彙的特性に関して言えば，その語のコロケーションを知っていなければならない。そしてその語を使用する適切な場所や対象となる相手についても正しく知っておく必要がある。

最後に，意味の面では，その語の意味の一般的な特性と特定の意味の範囲をそれぞれ知っていなければならない。語の意味の一般的な特性とは，例えば'man'という語では'male,' 'adult,' 'human being,' 'concrete,' 'animate'などである。これらの意味の特性は，その言語における他の多くの語と共有されている。

Cook（2001, p.62）は，語の習得は単に語形を翻訳された意味と結びつけることだけではなく，その語のspoken formとwritten form，文法構造における使用法とコロケーション，そして意味のいくつかの側面についての広範囲にわたる複雑な情報を習得することだとまとめている。

1.2 語を「知っている」と言うために必要な知識

これまでに見てきた諸家の所説に挙げられた語の知識をまとめると，以下の表の通りとなる。

表3. 語を「知っている」と言うために必要な知識

形	話し言葉	発音
	書き言葉	綴り
	語の構成要素	接辞と語幹
		その語のワード・ファミリーに含まれる語
意味	語形と意味	その語がどのような意味を表すか
		その語を表すためにどのような語形が使用されるか
		一般的な意味（components of the meaning / components theory）と特定の意味（prototype theory）
	概念と指示物	その語にはどのような概念が含まれているか
		その語の概念が表すのはどのような指示物か
	連想	同意関係（synonymy）
		包摂関係（hyponymy）
		全体・部分語関係（meronymy）
		反意関係（antonymy）
		動詞の上位・下位関係（troponymy）
		含意関係（entailment）
用法	文法的機能	品詞
		文法パタン
		特異な用法（名詞の不規則変化した複数形の綴りや発音などや可算名詞，不可算名詞の違いなど）
		動詞の項構造（argument structure）
	コロケーション	どのような語と連語をなすか
		サイズ（一連の語の並びに含まれる単語の数）
		タイプ（内容語と機能語の連語，および内容語と内容語の連語）
		連語関係にある語の親密さ
		連語関係にある語の可能な範囲
		慣用表現の一部，もしくは全体

| 用法における制約
（使用域や出現頻度） | どのような状況下で，およびどのような相手に対して，その語を使用するか
どのくらいの頻度で話し言葉／書き言葉に現れるか |

このように，ある語を「知っている」と言うためには，非常に多くの情報を持っていなければならないことになる。しかし，表3に挙げた情報のうち，1つ欠けたからといっても，その語を知らないということにはならない。Cook（2001, p.62）も，ある語の全ての側面を完全に知っている人は誰もいないと述べている。英語母語話者を含む誰もがそうであれば，ましてや日本人英語初学者が全ての情報を知っている必要はないと考えられる。それよりも基礎となる情報をきちんと学習し，学習段階を経るにつれて，徐々に情報を増やしていくことが望ましい。それゆえ，日本人英語初学者が語を「知っている」と言うために最低限知っておくべき情報を学習させることが有効であると考えられる。

　その基礎となる情報とは，語形，音形，項構造，そして通常最も普通に使われる意味とまず捉えておく。序章の冒頭で述べた通り，日本人英語初学者にとって必須な知識は，形（音声）とそれが表す意味の関係であり，所与の語（動詞）が典型的に持つ項構造，すなわち，その動詞がどのような文を生成するかということである。なぜならば日本人英語初学者がまず習得しなければならないのは，英語の基本構造だからである。

第 2 章　語彙リストの歴史的概観

　本章では，これまでの Graded readers を求める動きの中にあった歴史的語彙リスト（Basic English, GSL など）の考察と，その後の語彙リスト（竹蓋・中條，JACET 8000, The Longman Defining Vocabulary など）の共時的観点からの考察を行う。

2.1　Basic English

　C. K. Ogden によって提案された Basic English は，語の頻度や使用範囲などではなく，論理的，哲学的基準に基づいて構成され（Fries & Traver, 1950, p.50），英語学習の基本となる最小限の語彙を提供するためにデザインされたものである（Carter, 1998, p.23）。Basic English の850語は，OPERATIONS（100語），THINGS（600語），QUALITIES（150語）に分かれており，OPERATIONS の中に16語の動詞（*come, get, give, go, keep, let, make, put, seem, take, be, do, have, say, see, send*）が見られる（Carter & McCarthy, 1988, pp.4-5; 安藤他，1991, pp.592-593; Carter, 1998, pp.26-27）。しかし，安藤他（p.78）に，各語がその与えられた位置に固定されているわけではないと書かれていることや，語表の末尾に付記された SUMMARY OF RULES の中に「THINGS に属する300語の語尾に 'er', 'ing', 'ed' を付けることができる……'ing', 'ed' 付与の語形は，一般には動詞と目されている」とあることから，THINGS に挙げられた名詞のうち（位置が固定されていないのであれば OPERATIONS や QUALITIES の中の名詞の可能性もあるが）の300語に上記の接辞を付加して別の名詞や動詞を作ることも可能であると推測できる。それゆえ，16語よ

りも動詞の働きを表すことができるものが多くなると考えられる。その証拠として，Richards（1943, p.20 as cited in Carter, 1998, p.24）がBasic Englishを使って書いた文章を以下に示す：

> Basic English is English made simple by <u>limiting</u> the number of words to 850 and by <u>cutting</u> down the rules for <u>using</u> them to the smallest number necessary for the clear statement of ideas. And this is done without change in the normal order and behaviour of these words in everyday English. It is <u>limited</u> in its words and its rules but it keeps to the regular forms of English. And though it is <u>designed</u> to give the learner as little trouble as possible, it is no more strange to the eyes of my readers than these lines which are, in fact, in Basic English.（下線は筆者）

下線を施した動詞は，OPERATIONSに挙げられた動詞ではなく，THINGS (*design, limit, use*) とQUALITIES (*cut*) にそれぞれ見られる語である。
　SUMMARY OF RULESの中には，その他にも「形容詞に 'ly' を付けて副詞にする」（安藤他，1991, p.78）とあることや，「月の名（January, February, etc.），曜日の名（Monday, Tuesday, etc.），数詞（序数詞やonce, twice, half, quarterなども含む），擬音語（cuckoo, hiccup, etc.）」（安藤他，p.79）も850語以外に使用可能な語として挙げられていること，さらに「語表には出ていないが，'un' をQUALITIESの語頭に付けて反意語をつくっていいというルールもある……」（安藤他，p.78），「合成語は，'side + walk'→sidewalk, 'under + go'→undergo, 'how + ever'→howeverのようにかなり自由につくれる。」（安藤他，pp.78-79）などの記述から，これらの語を合わせると，Basic Englishとして使われる語彙の数は，実際には850語を遥かに超えることになる。
　上記の結果，Basic Englishが，850語という最小限の語彙による学習語彙リストではないことは明らかであるが，それでも明示された動詞が16語

しかないのでは，自然な英語を学習者に提供することは不可能だと考えられる。特に，put a question, have a desire for で言い換えが可能であるとの理由から *ask* や *want* をリストから省いているとあるが（Carter, 1998, p.25），1語の動詞で済むところをわざわざ複数の語句を用いて言い換えるのでは，学習者への負担も必要以上に多くなることが予想される。

　Basic Englishの創作者は，この850語を学習することがgeneral Englishへの基礎となるだろうと主張しているが，そのような拡充についての規則は挙げられていないうえ，それを促進するためにどのような学習解除が行われるべきか，また学習目標のためにBasic English systemの拡充性が学習目的のために効果的に等級に分けうるかなどが全く明白ではないとCarter（1998, p.25）は述べている。このように，学習した内容を，ある程度学習段階が進んだ後にわざわざ学習解除し，新たに別の「英語」を学習し直さなければならないということが学習を行う前から明らかなのであれば，Basic Englishを学ぶ目的が明確ではなくなる。

2.2　*A General Service List of English Words*

　高頻度語を収録した有名な語彙リストとして，Michael Westの *A General Service List of English Words*（1953）（以下GSLと略す）が挙げられる（Nation & Waring, 1997, p.14; Nation, 2001, p.11）。GSLには2,000語が収録されており，総語数500万語のコーパスから得られた，語の様々な意味と用法の出現頻度がカウントされている（West, 1953, vii）。全ての語が500万語のコーパスから得られたのではなく，中には250万語のコーパスから得られたものもあると書かれている。

　West（1953, ix）は，GSLに掲載された語のうち，1つの見出し語の語義が非常に異なる場合は，A-B-Cなどを付記し，それぞれを別語としてカウントすべきだと記している。それゆえ，それらを別語とカウントし，さらに1つの見出し語（例えばUSE）の中の語形が同じで，品詞が異なるもの

(use, v. と use, n.) も別語としてカウントした結果，GSLに記載された総異語数が4,574語であることが明らかになった。そのうち動詞は937語である。このように，4,574語の異語ごとに，それぞれの使用された割合をパーセンテージで示してあるリストは，現在でも類まれなものと言うことが可能である。さらに実際は異なる語源などにより，語形が同じでも語義が非常に異なる場合や，品詞が異なる場合も，それぞれの使用された割合をパーセンテージで示してあることは，当時のリストとしては極めて画期的だったと言える。

GSLについて，Nation and Waring (1997, p.13) は，以下のようにまとめている：

> *The General Service List* (West, 1953): The *GSL* contains 2,000 headwords and was developed in the 1940s. The frequency figures for most items are based on a 5,000,000 word written corpus. Percentage figures are given for different meanings and parts of speech of the headword. In spite of its age, some errors, and its solely written base, it still remains the best of the available lists because of its information about the frequency of each word's various meanings, and West's careful application of criteria other than frequency and range.

上記の通り，GSLに含まれたデータはやや古く，"The *GSL* was written so that it could be used as a resource for compiling simplified reading texts into stages or steps." (Nation & Waring, p.14) と書かれているように，GSLは，様々な読者層の段階に応じて簡易化された読本作成のための資料として使うために作成されたものなのである。

2.3 「現代英語のキーワード」

　竹蓋・中條（1994）は，「現代英語のキーワード」という語彙リストを開発し，その有効度の検証を行った。彼らの研究目的は，「今日の我が国の英語学習者のために『学習しやすく』，かつ，学習した結果の『実用効果が安定して高い』語彙リストを作成する」(p.3) ことであり，言語の表現は，そこに生活している「社会のシステム」や，その「時代の特質」に影響を受けるという考えに基づいて，現代社会を「情報化社会」，「国際化社会」，「女性の時代」と定義している (pp.3-4)。この語彙リストの使用対象者が「今日の我が国の英語学習者……」という記述の通り，あまりにも幅広いため，日本人英語学習者であれば学習段階がどれほど異なっていても構わないと考えられていると解釈できる。しかし，レベルが異なる学習者には，それぞれに異なる達成目標があると考えられ，その目標ごとに学ぶ内容や，必要となる語彙知識の深さは異なっているはずであるため，竹蓋・中條（1994）の語彙リストは必ずしも日本人英語初学者にとって有用であるとは言うことができない。

　また，竹蓋・中條 (1994, pp.4-5) は，語彙リスト作成の素材として，上記で定義した現代社会の中で「英語を母国語とする人たちが通常行うであろう言語活動」を記録した素材（生活語彙，専門分野［情報収集，ビジネス，会議，法律，コンピュータ］，日常会話，女性雑誌，テスト，米国教科書）を集め，この素材に「日本人が英語を学ぶにあたってとくに必要と考えられる種類の語彙（日本人の誤りやすい語）」と「最新の言語材料（科学技術関連の新語）」を補足したもの，作成された語彙リストの有効度を評価するための言語材料として「我が国の学習者がその外国語の目標とするであろう言語活動を，……23分野のものと定義した」もの，認知科学に基づいた学習の便を考慮するための「認知区分のための言語材料」の3種類を言語材料として収録している。

竹蓋・中條 (1994, p.8) は，「目標とする言語活動が定義されれば，その『言語活動で使われている語彙の何パーセントをカバーできるか』を観察することによって『有効度』が客観的に計測できるはずである」と述べている。つまり，竹蓋・中條の言う有効度とは，受容語彙としての有効度のみを示すものと定義することが可能である。竹蓋・中條のリストを見ると，有効度が94％，有効度のバラツキは標準偏差で4.5，未知語に遭遇する割合が16.8語に1語である。しかし，このように受容語彙としての有効度が高いことが，彼らが最初に挙げている「今日の我が国の英語学習者のために『学習しやすく』，かつ，学習した結果の『実用効果が安定して高い』語彙リスト」に相当するかどうかは疑問である。また未知語に遭遇する割合が低いことに関しては，比較に使用した言語材料が，いずれも竹蓋・中條の語彙リスト作成の資材にふさわしいものとして選ばれたことを考慮すれば（竹蓋・中條, p.5），そのような数値が出るのは当然だと考えられる。

2.4　『大学英語教育学会基本語リスト』

　『大学英語教育学会基本語リスト』（大学英語教育学会基本語改訂委員会, 2003）（以下JACET 8000と略す）は：

> （1）British National Corpus（BNC）から基準データを作成し，（2）JACET 8000サブコーパスデータと照合して8000語を選び出して順位を決め，（3）さらに8000語の順位を教育的観点から再調整する，という3つの段階で構成されている。(p.103)

このように大規模なコーパスとJACET 8000サブコーパスに基づいて作成されているため，このリストの語を学習すれば読み物を広くカバーでき，TOEICやTOEFLなど各種の検定試験にも有効で，オーラル・コミュニ

ケーション力を高める上でも有効とされている（pp.2-3）。しかし，JACET 8000の対象者が「小学生から一般社会人まで」(p.2)というのは，幅が広すぎると感じられる。

また，JACET 8000には，「Level 1からLevel 8を，それぞれアルファベット順に記載したリスト（pp.5-53）」（品詞情報あり）と，「JACET 8000のLevel 1を補完する250語をアルファベット順に記載したリスト(pp.55-56)」（品詞情報なし），そして「JACET 8000およびJACET 8000 plus 250の計8250語をアルファベット順に記載した総索引（pp.57-100)」（品詞情報なし）が掲載されている。レベル別リストには品詞情報が記してあるが，意味や用法についての記述は一切見られない。すると，このリストに挙げられた語を使用して教科書を作成したり，学習者に提示したりする際，意味や用法の頻度に関する情報が教授する側にも無いことになる。語形と品詞のみを選定してあっても，その語の持つ意味や用法が教授者によって異なれば，客観的な作業を通して作成した語彙リストの有効度が減少すると考えられる。また，学習者がJACET 8000を購入し，TOEICやTOEFLなどの検定試験に向けて語を覚えようとしても，意味と発音記号，用例などを辞書で調べ，自分にとって最も有用なものを選んで覚えなければならないという大きな負担も生じるだろう。それは小学生や中学生には現実的とは言い難い勉強法のように思われる。

また，「語源や品詞が異なる同形語であっても，別見出し語としない」（p.118）との表記の通り，JACET 8000では名詞と動詞の*bear*を1語にまとめて掲載している。しかし，Nation（2001, p.49）に "Homonyms should be counted and learned as different words, preferably at different times." とあるように，それぞれを別々に扱う方がよりスムーズに学習を進められると考えられる。語形が共通していれば品詞も語源も無視してまとめて1語とみなしたうえで頻度をカウントすれば，語彙リストの作成段階における手間は省けるが，正確さを欠くことになるだろう。

さらに，「連語・複合語などハイフンやスペースで2語（以上）にまた

がる語（句）は個々の単位に分割（p.119）」という表記の，特に複合語に関しては，複数の構成要素から1語をなしているものを要素ごとに分解することで，もともとの語としての出現頻度の意味をなさないことが考えられる。また，複数の構成要素のうち，いくつかの要素が語としての頻度が低いためにリストから削除される可能性もある。例えばJACET 8000では"amino acid"を *amino* と *acid* の2語としているが（p.119），同書（p.58）の挙げるそれぞれの語の出現頻度順位は，*amino* が6549位，*acid* が1530位となっている。この結果から，スペースで区切られてはいても1語の複合語である"amino acid"の出現頻度が無視されているということが明らかである。他にも類似の事例が散見される。

2.5 The Longman Defining Vocabulary

LDOCEでは，収録された全ての見出し語（106,000語）の定義をするために，約2,000語からなるThe Longman Defining Vocabularyが使用されている（Summers et al., 2003, p.1943）。LDOCEには，定義に使用された意味は，その定義語のリストに挙げられた語の最も一般的なもののみであり，リスト内の語のうち，品詞のラベルが付けられた語はその品詞としてのみで定義に使用されていることを示しているとの記述がある（Summers et al., p.1943）。

しかし，実際に定義語リストを概観して上記の内容に疑問を持ったため，筆者はLDOCEの編集長（Managing Editor）であるStephen Bullon氏と，監修者（Director）であるDella Summers氏に以下の質問をした：

（1）定義語の意味に関して，最も一般的な意味とは，各語の1番目の語義のみを指すのか
（2）品詞のラベル付けに関して，動詞以外では機能しない語のうち，*v* の表記があるものと無いものがあるが，品詞のラベル付け

に一貫性が無いのではないか
（3）定義語の"yellow"はLDOCEの見出し語として使用頻度に従って形容詞，名詞，動詞の順に掲載されている。最も使用頻度の低い動詞として定義語の役目を果たしているとは考え難いにも関わらず，*adj*や*n*という品詞のラベル付けがされていないという理由から，動詞としても使用されていると考えなければならないのか

そして以下のような回答を得た。

The answer to the first is that the "most common" meanings are not restricted to the first senses in each case, but possibly the first two or three. The very frequent words of the language have many senses which are very frequent, and we do not restrict ourselves to the first sense.

　Your question about the inconsistency in the annotation of word class labels is a good one. I have to admit that we have not been thoroughly consistent here. As rightly you observe, we do not use the verb "yellow" in any of our definitions. The list has been through several versions, and occasionally labels get lost, or aded [*sic*] to the wrong line of the list. I think we need to have another look at this before our next edition. (S. Bullon, personal communication, June 22, 2005)

Usually the first two meanings, occasionally the third meaning as well.

　I think it is mainly consistent, and the decision is made on the grounds of frequency, but probably one or two inconsistencies [*sic*] have not been corrected, such as the one for yellow that you mention below...

　I'm sure this is only every [*sic*] used as an adjective in the definitions. It should be marked as adj. (D. Summers, personal communication, July 4, 2005)

1つ目の質問に対し，Bullon（2005）およびSummers（2005）は共通して1番目と2番目，もしくは3番目までの語義を定義語の意味として採用したと述べている。LDOCEに収録された膨大な数の見出し語を定義するための定義語の語義を1つに制限することは不可能であり，この説明は的を射たものだと言うことができる。しかし，2つ目の質問に対してBullonは品詞のラベル付けが首尾一貫しておらず，版を重ねるごとにラベルが削除されたり，間違った場所に付加されたりしていることを認めている。一方Summersは，品詞のラベル付けにはいくらかの不一致はあるものの，出現頻度に基づいて行われているため大部分が一致していると主張している。常識的に考えて，"yellow"を定義語として扱う場合，その品詞は形容詞か名詞である。動詞としての用法が実在していても，一般性に欠けるため，動詞として定義語の役割を果たしているとは考え難い。そのように，一般常識的に考えれば，動詞としての用法で定義語として扱われないとわかるものが多数あるにも関わらず，LDOCEの編集関係者以外は，全ての定義語の用法や品詞を調べる以外にそれらがどの品詞で定義語として使用されているかを断定することはできないのである。それゆえ今後の改訂版で一貫性を持たせた品詞のラベル付けが行われることが期待される。

2.6 まとめ

本章で調査した語彙リストのうち，歴史的語彙リストは，Graded readersの作成に役立てるために作成されたことから，そこに挙げられた語彙を学習すれば何パーセントの語彙を知っていることになる，などのように学習後の出口を求めたものであった。読み物教材作成が目的であるため，資料が書き言葉のものに偏った，受容語彙を重視した形になることは仕方がないことかも知れない。

また，共時的観点から作成された竹蓋・中條（1994）やJACET 8000もまた，いわゆる出口側のリストと言うことができる。さらに，これらの語

彙リストの学習対象者が非常に幅広いことから，学習対象者は「誰でも良い」と受け取ることができる。数年間の英語学習を経験している高校生や大学生，さらに社会人では，学習者の興味・関心に関わる語彙や，学習者が専門としている分野の語彙を選ぶことに意義が見出せると考えられる。しかし，日本人英語初学者であれば，どのような場面でも，誰に対しても使用可能な，特殊化されない語彙群に触れる方が断然有益である。それゆえ，そのように異なる目的を持った幅広い人々を対象とするリスト自体には無理があると考えられる。

　The Longman Defining Vocabulary は，約2,000語という語数で，LDOCE に収録された全ての見出し語を定義することが可能であることから，馬本（2001）のいわゆる定義可能度[1]が高く，有用な語彙であると言うことができる。しかし，見出し語の定義語ということは，*adjective, adverb, noun, verb* などの辞書特有の表現において使用される語も多数含まれているため，たとえLDOCE自体が外国人英語学習者用の辞典であっても，定義語内の全ての語が英語教育に役立つ語であるとは必ずしも言うことはできない。

　日本人英語初学者に提案すべき語彙は，やはり「出口を意識した語彙」というよりは，英語の学習をその初期において円滑に進めるのに有効な語彙群，すなわち「入り口の語彙」である必要がある。

---

1) 馬本（2001, p.30）は，*Oxford English Dictionary* 第2版のCD-ROMの定義中に用いられた語を検索するDefinition Text Search機能を使用し，定義語としての頻度（他の語を定義する際に用いられる度合い）を定義可能度と呼んでいる。

第3章　動詞の捉え方

　本章では，本書で使用した資料である，The British component of the International Corpus of English, *Longman Grammar of Spoken and Written English* (Biber, Johansson, Leech, Conrad, & Finegan, 1999)，および*Longman Lexicon of Contemporary English* (McArthur, 1981)，それぞれの動詞の捉え方を紹介する。

3.1　The British component of the International Corpus of English

　The British component of the International Corpus of English（以下ICE-GBと略す）とは，1990年から1993年までの話し言葉60万語と書き言葉40万語のイギリス英語，約100万語を収録したコーパスであり，収録された全ての語に品詞のタグ付けが施され，文法的な分析が行われている（Nelson, Wallis, & Aarts, 2002, pp.4-5）。分析された文は図1に示した樹形図の形で見ることも可能である。

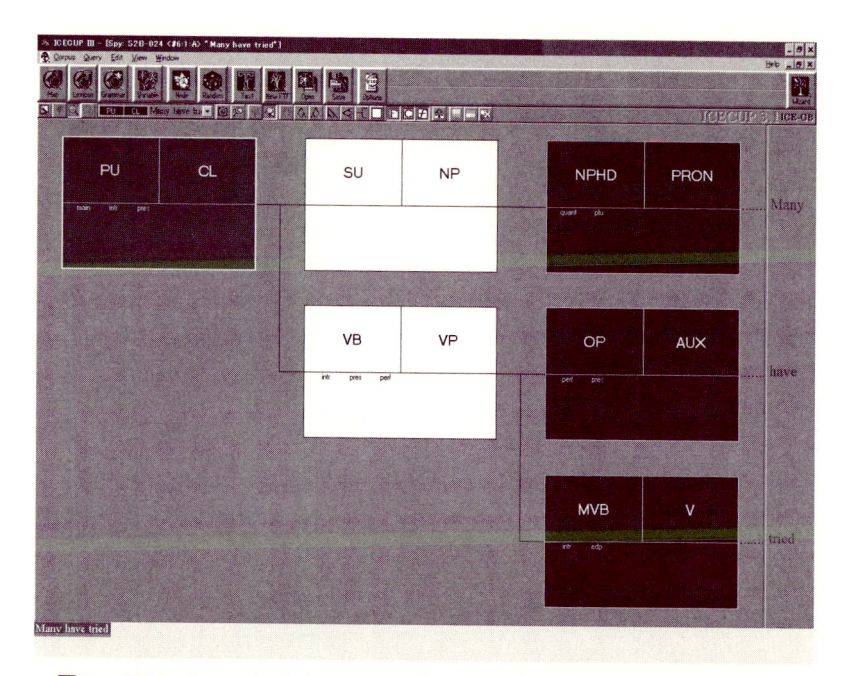

図1. *"Many have tried"*（*S2B-024 #6*）の樹形図（Nelson, Wallis, & Aarts, 2002, p.22の例をICE-GBからコピーしたもの）

樹形図の中の各node（節点）は，図2に見られるように3つの区分から成り立っている。

Function	Category (wordclass)
Feature[s]	

図2. The sectors of a node （Nelson, Wallis, & Aarts, 2002, p.22）

次にICE-GBのテキストカテゴリーとテキストコードの詳細を示す。

表4. Spoken Categories (Nelson, Wallis, & Aarts, 2002, p.307)

Text Categories	Textcodes
SPOKEN (300)	
Dialogue (180)	
Private (100)	
direct conversations (90)	S1A-001 to S1A-090
telephone calls (10)	S1A-091 to S1A-100
Public (80)	
classroom lessons (20)	S1B-001 to S1B-020
broadcast discussions (20)	S1B-021 to S1B-040
broadcast interviews (10)	S1B-041 to S1B-050
parliamentary debates (10)	S1B-051 to S1B-060
legal cross-examinations (10)	S1B-061 to S1B-070
business transactions (10)	S1B-071 to S1B-080
Monologue (120)	
Unscripted (70)	
spontaneous commentaries (20)	S2A-001 to S2A-020
unscripted speeches (30)	S2A-021 to S2A-050
demonstrations (10)	S2A-051 to S2A-060
legal presentations (10)	S2A-061 to S2A-070
Scripted (50)	
broadcast news (20)	S2B-001 to S2B-020
broadcast talks (20)	S2B-021 to S2B-040
non-broadcast talks (10)	S2B-041 to S2B-050

表5. Written Categories (Nelson, Wallis, & Aarts, 2002, p.308)

Text Categories	Textcodes
WRITTEN (200)	
Non-printed (50)	
students' untimed essays (10)	W1A-001 to W1A-010

students' examination scripts (10)	W1A-011 *to* W1A-020
social letters (15)	W1B-001 *to* W1B-015
business letters (15)	W1B-016 *to* W1B-030

Printed (150)
    Information Writing (100)

academic (40)	W2A-001 *to* W2A-040
popular (40)	W2B-001 *to* W2B-040
press reports (20)	W2C-001 *to* W2C-020

    Instructional Writing (20)

administrative / regulatory (10)	W2D-001 *to* W2D-010
skills & hobbies (10)	W2D-011 *to* W2D-020

    Persuasive Writing (10)

press editorials (10)	W2E-001 *to* W2E-010

    Creative Writing (20)

novels & stories (20)	W2F-001 *to* W2F-020

"S"で始まるコード (e.g., S1A-001) は，話し言葉のテクストであることを意味しており，"W"で始まるコード (e.g., W1A-001) は，書き言葉のテクストであることを意味している (Nelson, Wallis, & Aarts, 2002, pp.5-6)。

  ICE-GBの挙げるlexical verbsには，'v'の表記がされており，少なくとも2つのfeaturesがそれに続いている (Nelson, Wallis, & Aarts, 2002, p.38)。1つ目のfeatureは，complementation patternを示しており，ICE-GBには7つのパタンがある (表6参照)。2つ目のfeatureは，動詞の語形を示すもので，表6における 'tense / form' の中に見られるものである。clitic featuresは，lexical verbの "be" と "have" のみに適用されるものである (Nelson, Wallis, & Aarts, p.38)。

表6. ICE-GBの挙げる動詞のfeature（Nelson, Wallis, & Aarts, 2002, p.39）

class	feature	code
transitivity	intransitive	intr
	copular	cop
	monotransitive	montr
	dimonotransitive	dimontr
	ditransitive	ditr
	complex-transitive	cxtr
	transitive	trans
tense / form	present	pres
	past	past
	-ed participle	edp
	-ing participle	ingp
	infinitive	infin
clitics	enclitic	encl
	negative	neg

　ICE-GBで用いられる"ICE grammar"（Nelson, Wallis, & Aarts, 2002, pp.22-68）におけるtransitive（'trans'）以外のcomplementation patternは，Quirk et al.（1985, p.1170）に挙げられたものに準じている（Nelson, Wallis, & Aarts, p.38）。以下に各動詞のtransitivityについて詳細と例文を示す（Nelson, Wallis, & Aarts, pp.39-40）。各例文に付記されたテクストコード内の数字は，サブテクストを示している。例えばS1A-001-2はS1A-001の2番目のサブテクストである（Nelson, Wallis, & Aarts, p.6）。また例文前に付記した通し番号は，ここでの説明に限って使用しているデータ番号である。

　Intransitive verbs（'intr'）は目的語も補語も必要としない動詞である。この動詞の例文は，以下の通りである。

　　(1) ... life begins at forty [W2B-010 #230]　　　　　　V (intr, pres)

(2) You graduated in the summer... [S1A-034 #3]　　V (intr, past)

(3) Just don't know where to stop... [S1A-084 #235]　　V (intr, infin)

　Copular verbs ('cop') は主語補語を必要とするものである。例文からわかるように，副詞句も主語補語に含まれている。

(4) Food is available but not fuel to cook it with [S2B-005 #80]

V (cop, pres)

(5) Uh so you actually aren't a member of staff [S1B-062 #54]

V (cop, pres, neg)

(6) It's on the ground floor [S1A-073 #54]　　V (cop, pres, encl)

(7) Somehow he looks nice [S1A-065 #188]　　V (cop, pres)

(8) I felt quite ignorant [S1A-002 #83]　　V (cop, past)

(9) If anything it seems lighter [S1A-023 #164]　　V (cop, pres)

　Monotransitive verbs ('montr') は直接目的語のみを必要とするものである。

(10) I buy books all the time for work [S1A-013 #4]　　V (montr, pres)

(11) I used the wrong tactics [W2C-014 #106]　　V (montr, past)

(12) just... sign your name there [S1B-026 #160]　　V (montr, infin)

(13) Have you seen it [S1A-006 #103]　　V (montr, edp)

(14) I haven't a clue [S1B-080 #189]　　V (montr, pres, neg)

　Dimonotransitive verbs ('dimontr') は間接目的語のみを必要とするものである。

(15) ... when I asked her, she burst into tears [S1A-094 #110]

第 3 章　動詞の捉え方

(16) I'll tell you tomorrow [S1A-099 #396]　　V (dimontr, infin)
(17) Show me [S1A-042 #219]　　V (dimontr, infin)

※ (16) の上に V (dimontr, past) の表記あり

Ditransitive verbs（'ditr'）は間接目的語と直接目的語の両方を必要とするものである。

(18) We tell each other everything [S1A-054 #2]　　V (ditr, pres)
(19) So they built themselves a magnificent amphitheatre [S2B-027 #21]
　　　　　　　　　　　　　　　　　　　　　　　　V (ditr, past)
(20) Give us the answers [S1B-004 #156]　　V (ditr, infin)

Complex-transitive verbs（'cxtr'）は直接目的語と目的語補語を伴うものである。

(21) ... some people just find it very difficult [S1A-037 #31]
　　　　　　　　　　　　　　　　　　　　　　　　V (cxtr, pres)
(22) A glass of wine would make me incapable... [W2B-001 #51]
　　　　　　　　　　　　　　　　　　　　　　　　V (cxtr, infin)
(23) I hope you take that as a compliment [S1B-028 #93]　　V (cxtr, pres)

主要動詞が他動詞で，非定形節の主語もしくは主節の目的語になりうる名詞句を伴うような，transitivity の曖昧な動詞がいくつかある。それらには transitivity のタイプを 'V (trans, ...)' としてある。

(24) You wanted them to recognise your experience... [S1A-060 #151]
　　　　　　　　　　　　　　　　　　　　　　　　V (trans, past)
(25) I saw myself launching off into a philosophical treatise [S1A-001 #89]

39

(26) It is pleasure that makes you paint [S1B-008 #144]　　V (trans, past)
　　　　　　　　　　　　　　　　　　　　　　　　　　V (trans, pres)

　次に，本研究におけるICE-GBの動詞の抽出方法を述べる。まず，ICE-GBには動詞のカウント方法が2通りあるので，それについて説明する。
　1つ目はGrammaticonによる方法である。Grammaticonは，コーパス内のそれぞれに注釈付きのnodeを調査するのに役立ち，各語の機能と特徴を示すものである（Nelson, Wallis, & Aarts, 2002, p.210）。Grammaticon OptionsのNodeを"V"に設定し，検索を行うと，図3に見られるように語の機能，品詞，特性が示される。例えば図3に見られる"CJ, V (montr, infin)"はConjoin, Verb (monotransitive, infinitive) を意味している。

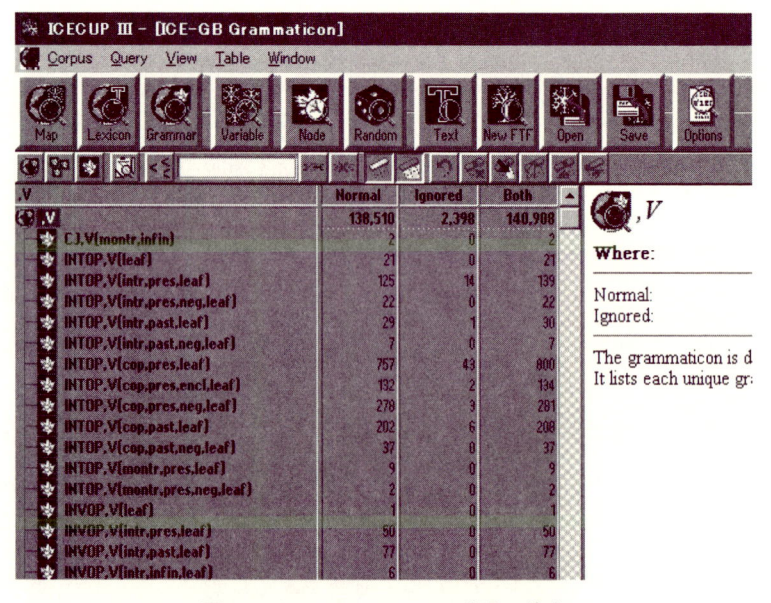

図3．Grammaticonによる動詞の検索

　上のCJ, V (montr, infin) の具体例は図4に示す通りである。

第 3 章　動詞の捉え方

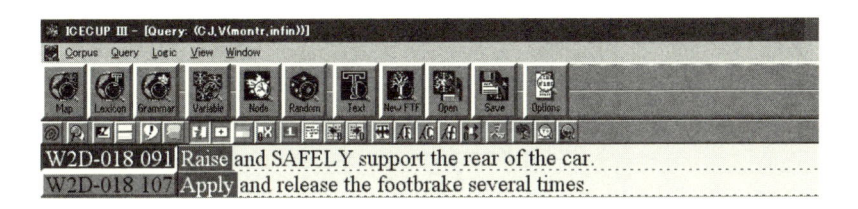

図 4．CJ, V (montr, infin) の動詞の具体例

網掛けされた "Raise" および "Apply" が，それぞれのテクスト内でこの用法を果たしているものである。

2 つ目は Lexicon による方法である。Lexicon は，コーパス内の辞書（語彙）的に異なる語と，それらの文法的な下位範疇を全て体系付けて表示するものである（Nelson, Wallis, & Aarts, 2002, p.206）。Lexicon Options から

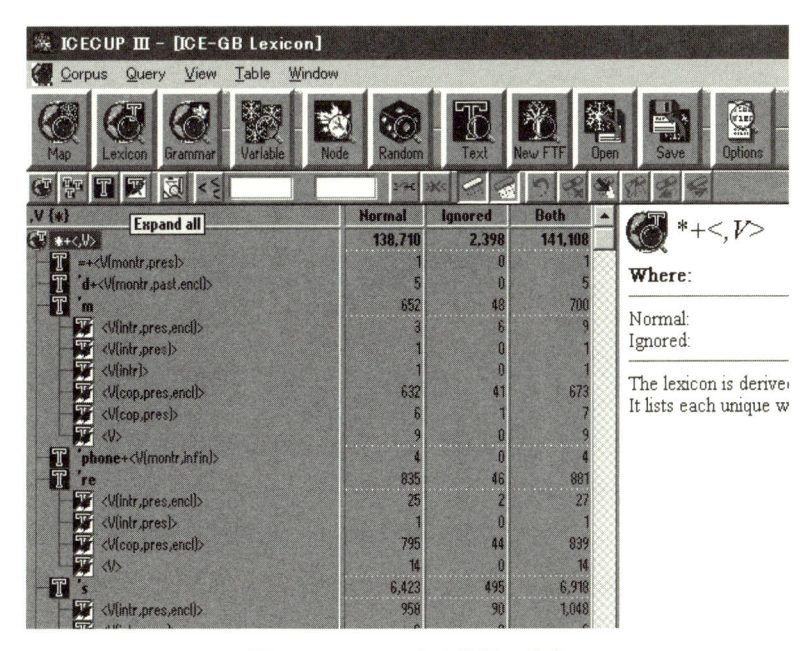

図 5．Lexicon による動詞の検索

Nodeを"V"，Wordを"*"に設定し動詞の検索を開始すると，ICE-GBの画面上には図5のように語彙項目がアルファベット順に示され，それぞれの語のtransitivityや現在形（presという表記），過去形（pastという表記）などのfeaturesが示される。これをコンピュータのハードディスクに保存し，Excelを選択して開くと表7のように表示される。

表7．ICE-GBのLexicon Optionsによる動詞（*+<,V>）の検索結果（一部抜粋）

	Normal	Ignored	Both
*+<,V>	138,710	2,398	141,108
= +<V(montr,pres)>	1	0	1
'd+<V(montr,past,encl)>	5	0	5
'm	652	48	700
<V(intr,pres,encl)>	3	6	9
<V(intr,pres)>	1	0	1
<V(intr)>	1	0	1
<V(cop,pres,encl)>	632	41	673
<V(cop,pres)>	6	1	7
<V>	9	0	9
'phone+<V(montr,infin)>	4	0	4
're	835	46	881
<V(intr,pres,encl)>	25	2	27
<V(intr,pres)>	1	0	1
<V(cop,pres,encl)>	795	44	839
<V>	14	0	14
's	6,423	495	6,918
<V(intr,pres,encl)>	958	90	1,048
<V(intr,pres)>	6	0	6
<V(intr)>	4	0	4
<V(cop,pres,encl)>	5,386	399	5,785
<V(cop,pres)>	19	1	20
<V(cop)>	1	0	1

<V(montr,pres,encl)>	2	0	2
<V>	47	5	52
<unclear-word>	8	0	8
<V(intr,pres)>	1	0	1
<V(intr,infin)>	2	0	2
<V(montr,edp)>	1	0	1
<V(montr,infin)>	4	0	4
've	33	2	35
<V(montr,pres,encl)>	30	2	32
<V(montr,pres)>	1	0	1
<V(trans,pres,encl)>	1	0	1
<V>	1	0	1
a-wooing+<V(intr,ingp)>	1	0	1
abandon+<V(montr,infin)>	4	0	4
abandoned	23	0	23
<V(montr,past)>	3	0	3
<V(montr,edp)>	19	0	19
<V>	1	0	1
abandoning+<V(montr,ingp)>	7	0	7
abbreviate+<V(montr,pres)>	1	0	1
abducted+<V(montr,edp)>	2	0	2

〜〜〜

write	207	1	208
<V(intr,pres)>	14	0	14
<V(intr,infin)>	94	0	94
<V(montr,pres)>	13	0	13
<V(montr,past)>	1	0	1
<V(montr,infin)>	80	1	81
<V(ditr,infin)>	3	0	3
<V(dimontr,infin)>	1	0	1
<V>	1	0	1
writes	8	0	8

<V(intr,pres)>	3	0	3
<V(montr,pres)>	4	0	4
<V>	1	0	1
writing	123	0	123
<V(intr,ingp)>	71	0	71
<V(montr,ingp)>	51	0	51
<V(ditr,ingp)>	1	0	1
written	151	0	151
<V(intr,edp)>	23	0	23
<V(intr,infin)>	1	0	1
<V(montr,edp)>	122	0	122
<V(cxtr,edp)>	4	0	4
<V>	1	0	1
wrong-footed+<V(montr,past)>	1	0	1
wrote	100	2	102
<V(intr,past)>	42	2	44
<V(montr,past)>	56	0	56
<V(ditr,past)>	1	0	1
<V(cxtr,past)>	1	0	1
x-rayed+<V(montr,edp)>	1	0	1
yawn	3	0	3
<V(intr,pres)>	1	0	1
<V(intr,infin)>	2	0	2
yawned+<V(intr,past)>	1	0	1
yawning+<V(intr,ingp)>	1	0	1
yearn	2	0	2
<V(intr,pres)>	1	0	1
<V(intr,infin)>	1	0	1
yearned+<V(intr,past)>	1	0	1
yearns	2	0	2
<V(intr,pres)>	1	0	1
<V(montr,pres)>	1	0	1
yelled+<V(intr,past)>	1	0	1
yelping+<V>	1	0	1

yield+<V(montr,infin)>	2	0	2
yielding+<V(montr,ingp)>	4	0	4
yields+<V(intr,pres)>	1	0	1
zeroing+<V(intr,ingp)>	1	0	1
zip+<V(intr,infin)>	1	0	1
zipped+<V(montr,past)>	1	0	1
zooming+<V(intr,ingp)>	1	0	1

表7から明らかなように，Lexiconでは具体的な語彙項目が示されているが，語形が異なれば別語として扱われているため，まず全ての動詞をtransitivityごとに分け，アルファベット順に並べた後に，そこに挙がった動詞の異形を全て原形にまとめる作業を行った。この手順を表7の"write"を用いて以下に示す。

write, writes, writing, written, wrote に挙げられたtransitivity（intr, montr, ditr, dimontr, cxtr, V）ごとに振り分け，各transitivityにおけるそれぞれを原形の"write"にまとめ，出現頻度の合計を求める。

 intr: *write* (108) + *writes* (3) + *writing* (71) + *written* (24) + *wrote* (42) =
  "write" (248)
 montr: *write* (94) + *writes* (4) + *writing* (51) + *written* (122) + *wrote* (56)
  = "write" (327)
 ditr: *write* (3) + *writing* (1) + *wrote* (1) = "write" (5)
 dimontr: *write* (1) = "write" (1)
 cxtr: *written* (4) + *wrote* (1) = "write" (5)
 V: *write* (1) + *writes* (1) + *written* (1) = "write" (3)

この作業により，付録1に挙げたICE-GBの動詞のリストを完成させた。上記の"write"のintransitiveの例に関しては，付録1のIntransitiveの表の17番目に"write"およびその出現頻度248を見ることができる。

このようにしてtransitivityごとに全ての動詞の原形とその出現頻度の合計を求めた。本書では，言い間違いや綴りミスなどの"Ignored"に含まれる動詞は扱わなかった。

上述の通り，ICE-GBでは2通りの語のカウント方法があるが，Grammaticonは，形態的には複数の語から構成され，意味的には1つの語のように機能するmulti-word unitにdittoというタグを付加し，これらをまとめて1語と数えているのに対し，Lexiconでは複数の要素を同じ品詞として機能する別語と数えている。例えばdittoタグ付きの"act as"は，コンピュータに保存した後，Excelで開くと以下のように表示される。

No <ADV(ge)> longer <ADV(ge,comp)> can <AUX(modal,pres)> any <PRON(nonass)> member <N(com,sing)> of <PREP(ge)> the <ART(def)> tribe <N(com,sing)> of <PREP(ge)> Levi <N(prop,sing)> <,> <PAUSE(short)> **act <V(cop,infin,ditto):1/2> as <V(cop,infin,ditto):2/2>** priest <N(com,sing)> <,> <PAUSE(short)>(S1B-001 #010:1:A)

（太字は筆者）

このように"act as"というcopularとして機能している動詞をGrammaticonでカウントすると1語であるのに対して，Lexiconでは"act"と"as"の2語とカウントされるうえ，"as"が単独でcopularのリストに現れる。本書では，複数の構成要素からなっても，1つの語として機能しているものは全て1語と扱うために，Grammaticonの挙げる数字を採用した。そのためLexiconで求めたtransitivityごとの動詞のリストから，dittoタグ付きのものを手作業で1語に直し，数を調整することとした。

dittoタグ付きの動詞に関して調査するために，New FTFというボタンをクリックして空白のFuzzy Tree Fragment（図6参照）を表示し，nodeのCategoryとして"V"を選択し，Feature(s)として"ditto"を選択して数を求め

る。すると図7に見られるように，dittoタグ付きの項目は黄色の下線で示され（Nelson, Wallis, & Aarts, 2002, p.24），199例存在していることが明らかとなった。

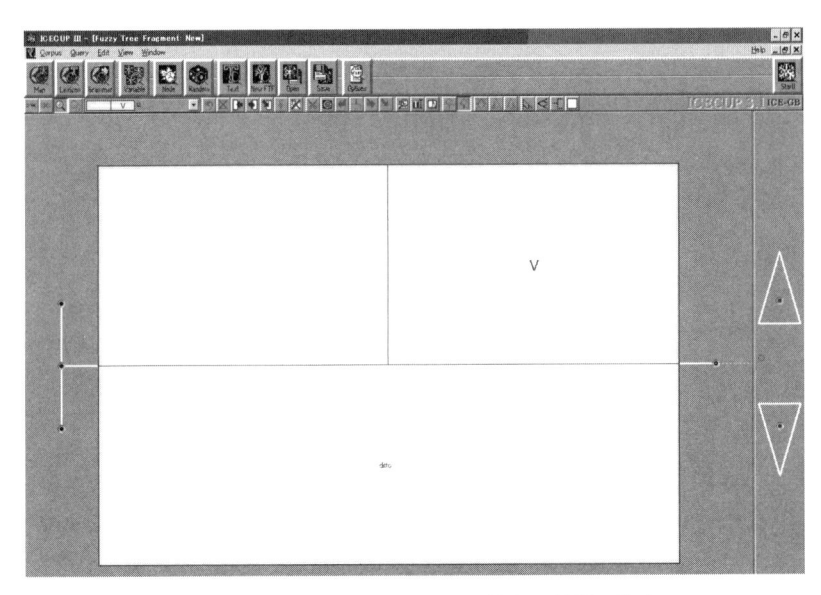

図6．New FTFによるdittoタグ付きの動詞の検索

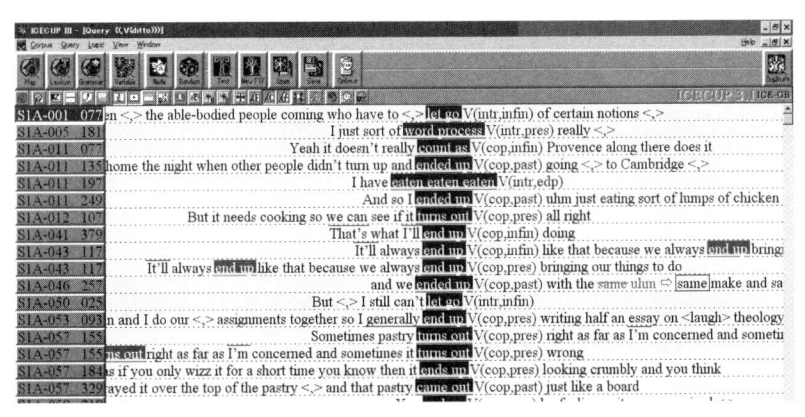

図7．New FTFにより求められたdittoタグ付きの動詞（一部）

これをコンピュータのハードディスクに保存し，Excelを選択して開き，さらにdittoタグ付きの動詞のみを取り出してアルファベット順に並べたものが表8である。

表8．dittoタグ付きの動詞199例

1	about <V(intr,infin,ditto):1/2> turn <V(intr,infin,ditto):2/2>	<:S2A-011 #107:1:A>
2	act <V(cop,infin,ditto):1/2> as <V(cop,infin,ditto):2/2>	<:W1A-006 #057:2>
3	act <V(cop,infin,ditto):1/2> as <V(cop,infin,ditto):2/2>	<:W2A-005 #098:1>
4	act <V(cop,infin,ditto):1/2> as <V(cop,infin,ditto):2/2>	<:W2A-010 #051:1>
5	act <V(cop,infin,ditto):1/2> as <V(cop,infin,ditto):2/2>	<:W2C-016 #055:2>
6	act <V(cop,infin,ditto):1/2> as <V(cop,infin,ditto):2/2>	<:S1B-001 #010:1:A>
7	act <V(cop,infin,ditto):1/2> as <V(cop,infin,ditto):2/2>	<:S1B-027 #118:1:C>
8	act <V(cop,infin,ditto):1/2> as <V(cop,infin,ditto):2/2>	<:S1B-030 #128:1:F>
9	act <V(cop,infin,ditto):1/2> as <V(cop,infin,ditto):2/2>	<:S2B-032 #095:2:A>
10	act <V(cop,infin,ditto):1/2> as <V(cop,infin,ditto):2/2>	<:W1A-009 #060:1>
11	act <V(cop,infin,ditto):1/2> as <V(cop,infin,ditto):2/2>	<:W2A-025 #065:1>
12	act <V(cop,infin,ditto):1/2> as <V(cop,infin,ditto):2/2>	<:W2C-001 #101:5>
13	act <V(cop,pres,ditto):1/2> as <V(cop,pres,ditto):2/2>	<:W2A-032 #072:1>
14	act <V(cop,pres,ditto):1/2> as <V(cop,pres,ditto):2/2>	<:W2A-035 #032:1>
15	act <V(cop,pres,ditto):1/2> as <V(cop,pres,ditto):2/2>	<:S2A-043 #120:1:A>
16	act <V(cop,pres,ditto):1/2> as <V(cop,pres,ditto):2/2>	<:W2A-035 #021:1>
17	act <V(cop,pres,ditto):1/2> as <V(cop,pres,ditto):2/2>	<:W2A-037 #092:1>
18	act <V(cop,pres,ditto):1/2> as <V(cop,pres,ditto):2/2>	<:W2B-027 #044:1>
19	act <V(cop,pres,ditto):1/2> as <V(cop,pres,ditto):2/2>	<:W2B-029 #045:1>
20	act <V(cop,pres,ditto):1/2> as <V(cop,pres,ditto):2/2>	<:W2B-029 #047:1>
21	act <V(cop,pres,ditto):1/2> as <V(cop,pres,ditto):2/2>	<:W2C-001 #076:4>
22	act <V(cop,pres,ditto):1/2> as <V(cop,pres,ditto):2/2>	<:W2D-007 #079:1>
23	acted <V(cop,past,ditto):1/2> as <V(cop,past,ditto):2/2>	<:W2B-003 #040:1>
24	acted <V(cop,past,ditto):1/2> as <V(cop,past,ditto):2/2>	<:W2C-020 #056:3>
25	acting <V(cop,ingp,ditto):1/2> as <V(cop,ingp,ditto):2/2>	<:W2F-014 #088:1>
26	acting <V(cop,ingp,ditto):1/2> as <V(cop,ingp,ditto):2/2>	<:S1B-014 #203:1:A>
27	acting <V(cop,ingp,ditto):1/2> as <V(cop,ingp,ditto):2/2>	<:S2B-015 #061:1:A>
28	Acting <V(cop,ingp,ditto):1/2> as <V(cop,ingp,ditto):2/2>	<:W1A-009 #073:1>
29	acting <V(cop,ingp,ditto):1/2> as <V(cop,ingp,ditto):2/2>	<:W1B-021 #016:1>
30	acting <V(cop,ingp,ditto):1/2> as <V(cop,ingp,ditto):2/2>	<:W2B-012 #027:1>

31	acts <V(cop,pres,ditto):1/2> as <V(cop,pres,ditto):2/2>	<:W1A-018 #109:2>
32	acts <V(cop,pres,ditto):1/2> as <V(cop,pres,ditto):2/2>	<:S2A-034 #112:4:A>
33	acts <V(cop,pres,ditto):1/2> as <V(cop,pres,ditto):2/2>	<:S2A-061 #043:1:A>
34	acts <V(cop,pres,ditto):1/2> as <V(cop,pres,ditto):2/2>	<:W1A-011 #085:2>
35	acts <V(cop,pres,ditto):1/2> as <V(cop,pres,ditto):2/2>	<:W1A-018 #092:2>
36	acts <V(cop,pres,ditto):1/2> as <V(cop,pres,ditto):2/2>	<:W2A-026 #045:1>
37	acts <V(cop,pres,ditto):1/2> as <V(cop,pres,ditto):2/2>	<:W2B-005 #009:1>
38	acts <V(cop,pres,ditto):1/2> as <V(cop,pres,ditto):2/2>	<:W2B-029 #084:1>
39	ad <V(montr,infin,ditto):1/2> lib <V(montr,infin,ditto):2/2>	<:S2A-029 #072:3:A>
40	amounts <V(cop,pres,ditto):1/2> to <V(cop,pres,ditto):2/2>	<:S1B-052 #020:1:D>
41	amounts <V(cop,pres,ditto):1/2> to <V(cop,pres,ditto):2/2>	<:S2B-016 #130:4:C>
42	avoid <V(montr,infin,ditto):1/2> / minimise <V(montr,infin,ditto):2/2>	<:W1A-009 #034:1>
43	back <V(intr,infin,ditto):1/2> space <V(intr,infin,ditto):2/2>	<:S1A-077 #307:1:A>
44	breast <V(intr,infin,ditto):1/2> beat <V(intr,infin,ditto):2/2>	<:S1B-043 #125:1:B>
45	butt <V(montr,edp,ditto):1/2> welded <V(montr,edp,ditto):2/2>	<:W2A-040 #057:1>
46	came <V(cop,past,ditto):1/2> out <V(cop,past,ditto):2/2>	<:S1A-057 #329:1:B>
47	chubb <V(montr,infin,ditto):1/2> lock <V(montr,infin,ditto):2/2>	<:W1B-007 #059:2>
48	code <V(cxtr,edp,ditto):1/2> named <V(cxtr,edp,ditto):2/2>	<:S2B-019 #049:1:F>
49	come <V(cop,edp,ditto):1/2> out <V(cop,edp,ditto):2/2>	<:S1B-046 #045:1:B>
50	come <V(cop,infin,ditto):1/2> out <V(cop,infin,ditto):2/2>	<:S1B-046 #046:1:B>
51	comes <V(cop,pres,ditto):1/2> in <V(cop,pres,ditto):2/2>	<:W2B-031 #038:1>
52	consist <V(cop,infin,ditto):1/2> of <V(cop,infin,ditto):2/2>	<:W2A-006 #094:1>
53	consisted <V(cop,past,ditto):1/2> of <V(cop,past,ditto):2/2>	<:S2A-048 #075:1:A>
54	consisted <V(cop,past,ditto):1/2> of <V(cop,past,ditto):2/2>	<:S1B-017 #036:1:A>
55	consisted <V(cop,past,ditto):1/2> of <V(cop,past,ditto):2/2>	<:W2A-006 #066:1>
56	consists <V(cop,pres,ditto):1/2> of <V(cop,pres,ditto):2/2>	<:S2A-025 #005:1:A>
57	count <V(cop,infin,ditto):1/2> as <V(cop,infin,ditto):2/2>	<:S1A-011 #077:1:B>
58	count <V(cop,pres,ditto):1/2> as <V(cop,pres,ditto):2/2>	<:S2B-044 #045:1:A>
59	counts <V(cop,pres,ditto):1/2> as <V(cop,pres,ditto):2/2>	<:S1A-066 #140:1:B>
60	counts <V(cop,pres,ditto):1/2> as <V(cop,pres,ditto):2/2>	<:W1B-007 #133:4>
61	'd <V(montr,past,encl,ditto):1/2> rather <V(montr,past,encl,ditto):2/2>	<:S1A-080 #078:1:B>
62	'd <V(montr,past,encl,ditto):1/2> rather <V(montr,past,encl,ditto):2/2>	<:S1A-080 #080:1:B>

63 diode <V(montr,edp,ditto):1/2> ORed   <:W2B-032 #047:1>
     <V(montr,edp,ditto):2/2>
64 drops <V(cop,pres,ditto):1/2> down <V(cop,pres,ditto):2/2>   <:S2A-017 #205:1:A>
65 eaten <V(intr,edp,ditto):1/3> eaten <V(intr,edp,ditto):2/3>   <:S1A-011 #197:2:A>
     eaten <V(intr,edp,ditto):3/3>
66 emphasised <V(montr,edp,ditto):1/2> / reiterated   <:W1A-009 #066:1>
     <V(montr,edp,ditto):2/2>
67 empire <V(intr,infin,ditto):1/2> build <V(intr,infin,ditto):2/2>   <:W1B-029 #051:2>
68 end <V(cop,infin,ditto):1/2> up <V(cop,infin,ditto):2/2>   <:S1A-072 #193:1:B>
69 end <V(cop,infin,ditto):1/2> up <V(cop,infin,ditto):2/2>   <:S1A-041 #379:1:A>
70 end <V(cop,infin,ditto):1/2> up <V(cop,infin,ditto):2/2>   <:S1A-043 #117:1:B>
71 end <V(cop,infin,ditto):1/2> up <V(cop,infin,ditto):2/2>   <:S1A-072 #087:1:A>
72 end <V(cop,infin,ditto):1/2> up <V(cop,infin,ditto):2/2>   <:S1A-085 #009:1:B>
73 end <V(cop,infin,ditto):1/2> up <V(cop,infin,ditto):2/2>   <:S1A-095 #040:1:B>
74 end <V(cop,infin,ditto):1/2> up <V(cop,infin,ditto):2/2>   <:S1A-095 #094:1:A>
75 end <V(cop,infin,ditto):1/2> up <V(cop,infin,ditto):2/2>   <:S1A-097 #118:1:A>
76 end <V(cop,infin,ditto):1/2> up <V(cop,infin,ditto):2/2>   <:S1B-018 #153:1:F>
77 end <V(cop,infin,ditto):1/2> up <V(cop,infin,ditto):2/2>   <:S1B-033 #020:1:C>
78 end <V(cop,infin,ditto):1/2> up <V(cop,infin,ditto):2/2>   <:S1B-036 #060:1:E>
79 end <V(cop,infin,ditto):1/2> up <V(cop,infin,ditto):2/2>   <:S1B-074 #301:3:C>
80 end <V(cop,infin,ditto):1/2> up <V(cop,infin,ditto):2/2>   <:S2A-029 #121:3:A>
81 end <V(cop,infin,ditto):1/2> up <V(cop,infin,ditto):2/2>   <:W2B-001 #082:1>
82 end <V(cop,infin,ditto):1/2> up <V(cop,infin,ditto):2/2>   <:W2F-007 #132:1>
83 end <V(cop,pres,ditto):1/2> up <V(cop,pres,ditto):2/2>   <:S1B-078 #036:1:B>
84 end <V(cop,pres,ditto):1/2> up <V(cop,pres,ditto):2/2>   <:S2A-029 #113:3:A>
85 end <V(cop,pres,ditto):1/2> up <V(cop,pres,ditto):2/2>   <:S1A-043 #117:1:B>
86 end <V(cop,pres,ditto):1/2> up <V(cop,pres,ditto):2/2>   <:S1A-053 #093:1:B>
87 end <V(cop,pres,ditto):1/2> up <V(cop,pres,ditto):2/2>   <:S1A-058 #218:3:B>
88 end <V(cop,pres,ditto):1/2> up <V(cop,pres,ditto):2/2>   <:S1A-096 #030:1:B>
89 end <V(cop,pres,ditto):1/2> up <V(cop,pres,ditto):2/2>   <:S2A-034 #051:2:A>
90 end <V(cop,pres,ditto):1/2> up <V(cop,pres,ditto):2/2>   <:W2D-011 #083:1>
91 end <V(cop,pres,ditto):1/2> up <V(cop,pres,ditto):2/2>   <:W2D-015 #040:1>
92 end <V(ditto):1/2> up <V(ditto):2/2>   <:S1B-060 #080:1:D>
93 ended <V(cop,edp,ditto):1/2> up <V(cop,edp,ditto):2/2>   <:W1B-006 #039:1>
94 ended <V(cop,edp,ditto):1/2> up <V(cop,edp,ditto):2/2>   <:W1B-007 #009:1>
95 ended <V(cop,past,ditto):1/2> up <V(cop,past,ditto):2/2>   <:W1B-007 #101:3>
96 ended <V(cop,past,ditto):1/2> up <V(cop,past,ditto):2/2>   <:S1A-011 #135:2:A>

第 3 章　動詞の捉え方

97	ended <V(cop,past,ditto):1/2> up <V(cop,past,ditto):2/2>	<:S1A-011 #249:2:B>
98	ended <V(cop,past,ditto):1/2> up <V(cop,past,ditto):2/2>	<:S1A-046 #257:1:C>
99	ended <V(cop,past,ditto):1/2> up <V(cop,past,ditto):2/2>	<:S1B-078 #013:1:B>
100	ended <V(cop,past,ditto):1/2> up <V(cop,past,ditto):2/2>	<:W1B-007 #043:2>
101	ended <V(cop,past,ditto):1/2> up <V(cop,past,ditto):2/2>	<:W1B-011 #007:1>
102	ended <V(cop,past,ditto):1/2> up <V(cop,past,ditto):2/2>	<:W1B-013 #066:2>
103	ended <V(cop,past,ditto):1/2> up <V(cop,past,ditto):2/2>	<:W2B-012 #110:1>
104	ending <V(cop,ingp,ditto):1/2> up <V(cop,ingp,ditto):2/2>	<:S1B-008 #125:2:A>
105	ends <V(cop,pres,ditto):1/2> up <V(cop,pres,ditto):2/2>	<:S1B-030 #138:1:F>
106	ends <V(cop,pres,ditto):1/2> up <V(cop,pres,ditto):2/2>	<:W2A-004 #039:1>
107	ends <V(cop,pres,ditto):1/2> up <V(cop,pres,ditto):2/2>	<:W2D-013 #130:1>
108	ends <V(cop,pres,ditto):1/2> up <V(cop,pres,ditto):2/2>	<:S1A-057 #184:1:A>
109	ends <V(cop,pres,ditto):1/2> up <V(cop,pres,ditto):2/2>	<:S2A-017 #169:1:A>
110	ends <V(cop,pres,ditto):1/2> up <V(cop,pres,ditto):2/2>	<:S2B-028 #009:1:A>
111	ends <V(cop,pres,ditto):1/2> up <V(cop,pres,ditto):2/2>	<:W2B-028 #056:1>
112	gold <V(montr,edp,ditto):1/2> coated <V(montr,edp,ditto):2/2>	<:W2A-028 #044:1>
113	hand <V(montr,past,ditto):1/2> reared <V(montr,past,ditto):2/2>	<:W1B-014 #104:5>
114	inside <V(montr,pres,ditto):1/2> edges <V(montr,pres,ditto):2/2>	<:S2A-013 #115:3:A>
115	let <V(intr,infin,ditto):1/2> go <V(intr,infin,ditto):2/2>	<:S1A-001 #077:1:B>
116	let <V(intr,infin,ditto):1/2> go <V(intr,infin,ditto):2/2>	<:S1A-050 #025:1:B>
117	let <V(intr,infin,ditto):1/2> go <V(intr,infin,ditto):2/2>	<:S2A-008 #155:5:A>
118	let <V(intr,infin,ditto):1/2> go <V(intr,infin,ditto):2/2>	<:S2A-054 #052:1:A>
119	Let <V(intr,infin,ditto):1/2> go <V(intr,infin,ditto):2/2>	<:W2F-008 #138:1>
120	listen <V(intr,infin,ditto):1/3> listen <V(intr,infin,ditto):2/3> listen <V(intr,infin,ditto):3/3>	<:S1A-092 #335:1:A>
121	make <V(cop,infin,ditto):1/2> up <V(cop,infin,ditto):2/2>	<:S1B-015 #165:1:A>
122	make <V(cop,infin,ditto):1/2> up <V(cop,infin,ditto):2/2>	<:S1B-062 #131:1:B>
123	make <V(cop,pres,ditto):1/2> up <V(cop,pres,ditto):2/2>	<:W2D-005 #129:1>
124	make <V(cop,pres,ditto):1/2> up <V(cop,pres,ditto):2/2>	<:S1B-015 #033:1:A>
125	make <V(cop,pres,ditto):1/2> up <V(cop,pres,ditto):2/2>	<:S1B-022 #004:1:A>
126	make <V(cop,pres,ditto):1/2> up <V(cop,pres,ditto):2/2>	<:S1B-036 #050:1:E>
127	make <V(cop,pres,ditto):1/2> up <V(cop,pres,ditto):2/2>	<:S2B-039 #041:2:A>
128	make <V(cop,pres,ditto):1/2> up <V(cop,pres,ditto):2/2>	<:S2B-040 #011:1:A>
129	make <V(cop,pres,ditto):1/2> up <V(cop,pres,ditto):2/2>	<:W2A-019 #079:1>

130	make <V(cop,pres,ditto):1/2> up <V(cop,pres,ditto):2/2>	<:W2B-007 #029:1>
131	make <V(cop,pres,ditto):1/2> up <V(cop,pres,ditto):2/2>	<:W2B-031 #025:1>
132	make <V(cop,pres,ditto):1/2> up <V(cop,pres,ditto):2/2>	<:W2B-031 #026:1>
133	make <V(cop,pres,ditto):1/2> up <V(cop,pres,ditto):2/2>	<:W2B-039 #082:1>
134	make <V(intr,infin,ditto):1/2> do <V(intr,infin,ditto):2/2>	<:W2D-017 #065:1>
135	makes <V(cop,pres,ditto):1/2> up <V(cop,pres,ditto):2/2>	<:S1B-015 #038:1:A>
136	makes <V(cop,pres,ditto):1/2> up <V(cop,pres,ditto):2/2>	<:S2B-049 #043:1:A>
137	makes <V(cop,pres,ditto):1/2> up <V(cop,pres,ditto):2/2>	<:W1A-008 #058:1>
138	makes <V(cop,pres,ditto):1/2> up <V(cop,pres,ditto):2/2>	<:W2B-030 #047:1>
139	making <V(cop,ingp,ditto):1/2> up <V(cop,ingp,ditto):2/2>	<:S1B-062 #060:1:C>
140	march <V(intr,pres,ditto):1/2> past <V(intr,pres,ditto):2/2>	<:S2A-011 #028:1:A>
141	march <V(intr,pres,ditto):1/2> past <V(intr,pres,ditto):2/2>	<:S2A-011 #030:1:A>
142	mass <V(montr,edp,ditto):1/2> produced <V(montr,edp,ditto):2/2>	<:W1A-019 #044:2>
143	mass <V(montr,edp,ditto):1/2> produced <V(montr,edp,ditto):2/2>	<:W1A-019 #087:4>
144	mass <V(montr,infin,ditto):1/2> mobilise <V(montr,infin,ditto):2/2>	<:W2A-017 #003:1>
145	misled <V(ditto):1/2> confused <V(ditto):2/2>	<:S1B-060 #092:2:D>
146	Mountain <V(montr,infin,ditto):1/2> fold <V(montr,infin,ditto):2/2>	<:W2D-019 #056:1>
147	Mountain <V(montr,infin,ditto):1/2> fold <V(montr,infin,ditto):2/2>	<:W2D-019 #079:1>
148	occured <V(intr,past,ditto):1/2> occurred <V(intr,past,ditto):2/2>	<:W1A-003 #102:1>
149	Outside <V(montr,infin,ditto):1/2> reverse <V(montr,infin,ditto):2/2>	<:W2D-019 #166:1>
150	oven <V(intr,ingp,ditto):1/2> baking <V(intr,ingp,ditto):2/2>	<:W2D-020 #054:1>
151	poll <V(montr,edp,ditto):1/3> tax <V(montr,edp,ditto):2/3> capped <V(montr,edp,ditto):3/3>	<:S2B-030 #135:4:A>
152	poses <V(cop,pres,ditto):1/2> as <V(cop,pres,ditto):2/2>	<:W1A-010 #094:1>
153	put <V(intr,edp,ditto):1/2> paid <V(intr,edp,ditto):2/2>	<:S2B-039 #080:3:A>
154	quick <V(intr,pres,ditto):1/2> march <V(intr,pres,ditto):2/2>	<:S2A-011 #114:1:A>
155	rate <V(montr,edp,ditto):1/2> capped <V(montr,edp,ditto):2/2>	<:S2B-030 #137:4:A>
156	rawl <V(montr,edp,ditto):1/2> bolted <V(montr,edp,ditto):2/2>	<:W2A-040 #057:1>

第 3 章　動詞の捉え方

157　return <V(montr,edp,ditto):1/2> folded　　　　　　　　　　<:W2A-040 #059:1>
　　　<V(montr,edp,ditto):2/2>
158　right <V(intr,ingp,ditto):1/2> footing <V(intr,ingp,ditto):2/2> <:S2A-017 #009:1:A>
159　Right <V(intr,past,ditto):1/2> footed <V(intr,past,ditto):2/2> <:S2A-001 #023:1:A>
160　roller <V(intr,ingp,ditto):1/2> skating　　　　　　　　　　<:W1B-012 #062:1>
　　　<V(intr,ingp,ditto):2/2>
161　row/column <V(intr,ingp,ditto):1/2> scanning　　　　　　<:W2B-039 #108:1>
　　　<V(intr,ingp,ditto):2/2>
162　serve <V(cop,infin,ditto):1/2> as <V(cop,infin,ditto):2/2> <:W2B-020 #056:1>
163　serve <V(cop,infin,ditto):1/2> as <V(cop,infin,ditto):2/2> <:S2B-029 #148:1:A>
164　serve <V(cop,infin,ditto):1/2> as <V(cop,infin,ditto):2/2> <:S2B-050 #009:1:A>
165　serve <V(cop,infin,ditto):1/2> as <V(cop,infin,ditto):2/2> <:S2B-050 #018:1:A>
166　serve <V(cop,infin,ditto):1/2> as <V(cop,infin,ditto):2/2> <:W2A-020 #032:1>
167　serve <V(cop,pres,ditto):1/2> as <V(cop,pres,ditto):2/2> <:W1A-007 #012:1>
168　served <V(cop,edp,ditto):1/2> as <V(cop,edp,ditto):2/2> <:S2A-011 #125:1:A>
169　served <V(cop,past,ditto):1/2> as <V(cop,past,ditto):2/2> <:S2A-019 #056:1:A>
170　served <V(cop,past,ditto):1/2> as <V(cop,past,ditto):2/2> <:S2B-043 #042:1:A>
171　served <V(cop,past,ditto):1/2> as <V(cop,past,ditto):2/2> <:W2B-004 #120:1>
172　serves <V(cop,pres,ditto):1/2> as <V(cop,pres,ditto):2/2> <:S2B-033 #045:1:A>
173　serves <V(cop,pres,ditto):1/2> as <V(cop,pres,ditto):2/2> <:W2D-003 #029:1>
174　shallow <V(intr,infin,ditto):1/2> fry <V(intr,infin,ditto):2/2> <:W2D-020 #069:1>
175　short <V(montr,infin,ditto):1/2> circuit　　　　　　　　　<:W2A-014 #068:1>
　　　<V(montr,infin,ditto):2/2>
176　sitting <V(intr,ingp,ditto):1/2> saying　　　　　　　　　　<:S1A-092 #340:1:A>
　　　<V(intr,ingp,ditto):2/2>
177　slow <V(intr,pres,ditto):1/2> march <V(intr,pres,ditto):2/2> <:S2A-011 #067:1:A>
178　slow <V(intr,pres,ditto):1/2> march <V(intr,pres,ditto):2/2> <:S2A-011 #075:1:A>
179　steam <V(montr,edp,ditto):1/2> rolled　　　　　　　　　　<:S1B-008 #049:2:A>
　　　<V(montr,edp,ditto):2/2>
180　triple <V(intr,infin,ditto):1/2> check <V(intr,infin,ditto):2/2> <:S1A-096 #240:1:B>
181　turn <V(cop,infin,ditto):1/2> into <V(cop,infin,ditto):2/2> <:W2E-003 #038:1>
182　turn <V(cop,infin,ditto):1/2> out <V(cop,infin,ditto):2/2> <:S1A-085 #040:1:B>
183　turn <V(cop,infin,ditto):1/2> out <V(cop,infin,ditto):2/2> <:S1B-016 #127:1:C>
184　turn <V(cop,infin,ditto):1/2> out <V(cop,infin,ditto):2/2> <:S1B-049 #011:1:A>
185　turned <V(cop,edp,ditto):1/2> out <V(cop,edp,ditto):2/2> <:W1B-008 #145:5>
186　turned <V(cop,edp,ditto):1/2> out <V(cop,edp,ditto):2/2> <:S2A-027 #040:1:A>
187　turned <V(cop,edp,ditto):1/2> out <V(cop,edp,ditto):2/2> <:W2B-004 #045:1>

53

188	turned <V(cop,past,ditto):1/2> out <V(cop,past,ditto):2/2>			<:W1B-029 #097:4>
189	turns <V(cop,pres,ditto):1/2> out <V(cop,pres,ditto):2/2>			<:S1A-012 #107:1:B>
190	turns <V(cop,pres,ditto):1/2> out <V(cop,pres,ditto):2/2>			<:S1A-057 #155:1:A>
191	turns <V(cop,pres,ditto):1/2> out <V(cop,pres,ditto):2/2>			<:S1A-057 #155:1:A>
192	turns <V(cop,pres,ditto):1/2> out <V(cop,pres,ditto):2/2>			<:S1B-018 #129:1:F>
193	turns <V(cop,pres,ditto):1/2> out <V(cop,pres,ditto):2/2>			<:S1B-042 #129:1:B>
194	word <V(intr,ingp,ditto):1/2> processing <V(intr,ingp,ditto):2/2>			<:W2B-039 #027:1>
195	word <V(intr,ingp,ditto):1/2> processing <V(intr,ingp,ditto):2/2>			<:W2B-039 #070:1>
196	word <V(intr,ingp,ditto):1/2> processing <V(intr,ingp,ditto):2/2>			<:W2B-039 #071:1>
197	word <V(intr,ingp,ditto):1/2> processing <V(intr,ingp,ditto):2/2>			<:W2B-039 #076:1>
198	word <V(intr,pres,ditto):1/2> process <V(intr,pres,ditto):2/2>			<:S1A-005 #181:1:B>
199	word <V(montr,ingp,ditto):1/2> processing <V(montr,ingp,ditto):2/2>			<:W1B-004 #004:1>

そしてtransitivityごとに動詞の異形を原形にまとめる．表8に挙げた*act as, acted as, acting as, acts as*を例に取ると，以下のようになる．

cop: *act as* (21) + *acted as* (2) + *acting as* (6) + *acts as* (8) = "act as" (37)

この方法で得られたdittoタグ付きの動詞は，表9に示す通りである．

表9．dittoタグ付きの動詞のtransitivityと出現頻度

	dittoタグ付きの動詞		transitivity	頻度
1	act	as	cop	37
2	amount	to	cop	2
3	come	out	cop	3
4	come	in	cop	1

5	consist	of		cop	5
6	count	as		cop	4
7	drop	down		cop	1
8	end	up		cop	43
9	make	up		cop	18
10	pose	as		cop	1
11	serve	as		cop	12
12	turn	into		cop	1
13	turn	out		cop	12
14	code	name		cxtr	1
15	about	turn		intr	1
16	back	space		intr	1
17	breast	beat		intr	1
18	eat	eat	eat	intr	1
19	empire	build		intr	1
20	let	go		intr	5
21	listen	listen	listen	intr	1
22	make	do		intr	1
23	march	past		intr	2
24	occur	occur		intr	1
25	oven	bake		intr	1
26	put	pay		intr	1
27	quick	march		intr	1
28	right	foot		intr	2
29	roller	skate		intr	1
30	row / column	scan		intr	1
31	shallow	fry		intr	1
32	sit	say		intr	1
33	slow	march		intr	2
34	triple	check		intr	1
35	word	process		intr	5
36	ad	lib		montr	1
37	avoid	/ minimise		montr	1
38	butt	weld		montr	1

55

39	chubb	lock		montr	1
40	have	rather		montr	2
41	diode	OR		montr	1
42	emphasise	/ reiterate		montr	1
43	gold	coat		montr	1
44	hand	rear		montr	1
45	inside	edge		montr	1
46	mass	produce		montr	2
47	mass	mobilise		montr	1
48	mountain	fold		montr	2
49	outside	reverse		montr	1
50	poll	tax	cap	montr	1
51	rate	cap		montr	1
52	rawl	bolt		montr	1
53	return	fold		montr	1
54	short	circuit		montr	1
55	steam	roll		montr	1
56	word	process		montr	1
57	end	up		unspecified	1
58	mislead	confuse		unspecified	1
				合計	199

表9に現れる動詞を先にLexiconで得た各transitivityの動詞の原形のリストから削除し，別語としてdittoタグ付きの動詞を独立した語彙項目としてリストに付け加えた。その方法を"act as"を用いて表10に例示する。copularのリストに挙がっているact（41）とas（54）のそれぞれから，"act as"（37）の構成要素として現れるものを引いてact（4），as（17）とし，"act as"を単独の語としてリストに加えた。

第3章　動詞の捉え方

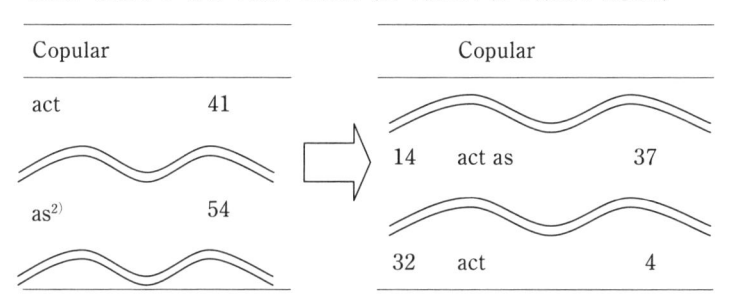

表10．dittoタグ付きの動詞の整理（右の欄は本書の付録1を参照）

Copular		Copular	
act	41	14　act as	37
as[2)]	54	32　act	4

　この結果，各transitivityに挙げられた動詞の合計は，Grammaticonが挙げるものよりも3語少ない138,507語となった。この数から，ICE-GBにおいて動詞として機能をしてはいるものの，いずれのtransitivityにも明確に分類ができない<unspecified>に属するものの総語数および異語数は動詞全体のそれぞれから排除した。そのため，本書で使用した動詞の総語数は137,590語となった。ICE-GBの挙げるtransitivityごとの動詞の数は以下の表の通りである。

表11．ICE-GBにおける動詞のTransitivityごとの総語数，異語数と異語数の割合

Transitivity	総語数	異語数	異語数の割合（%）
intransitive	32,357	1,710	33.09
copular	31,740	61	1.18
monotransitive	64,486	2,752	53.26
dimonotransitive	271	24	0.46
ditransitive	1,803	87	1.68
complex-transitive	4,235	371	7.18
transitive	2,698	162	3.14
Total	137,590	5,167	99.99

2）asはact以外の動詞とも結びついて語をなすため，この作業後，単独で動詞としてリスト内に現れることはない。

57

ICE-GBの動詞の総語数137,590語における総異語数は5,167語であるが，1つの動詞が複数のtransitivityに現れる場合，それぞれを1語とカウントしているため，用法を無視して全体の語形のみを見た場合は，異語数が3,473語となる。

1億語を収録しているBritish National Corpus（BNC）と比較すると，ICE-GBの収録語数は100万語と少ないが，データの9割が書き言葉の資料であるBNCとは違い，ICE-GBは話し言葉のコーパス（テキスト数300）と書き言葉のコーパス（テキスト数200）をバランス良く扱っており，また全てのテクスト・ユニット（文）が機能と範疇のレベルで統語的に構文解析されているため，本研究の資料として使用した。

ICE-GBの動詞のデータをtransitivityごとにまとめたものを付録1に示す。ICE-GBではこれらデータを頻度順に整理することができるので，全てのコーパス内の動詞についてその作業を行った。

3.2 *Longman Grammar of Spoken and Written English*

Longman Grammar of Spoken and Written English（Biber, Johansson, Leech, Conrad, & Finegan, 1999）（以下LGSWEと略す）は，動詞をmain verbとauxiliary verbの役割によってlexical verbs（*run, eat*など），primary verbs（*be, have, do*），modal verbs（*can, will, might*など）の3つの主要クラスに分類している（Biber et al., 1999, p.358）。また，そのような分類方法に加え，動詞の意味領域（semantic domain），および統合価パタン（valency pattern）に基づく分類も行っている。

LGSWEでは，動詞を7つの主要な意味領域（activity verbs, communication verbs, mental verbs, causative verbs, verbs of simple occurrence, verbs of existence or relationship, aspectual verbs）に分類している（Biber et al., 1999, p.360）。以下に各動詞の説明と，それぞれの動詞を使った例文を示す。以下の例文に付記した通し番号は，ここでの説明に限って使用しているデータ番号であ

る。各例文の後ろに付記している記号（CONV, FICT, NEWS, ACAD）は，それぞれ conversation transcription, fiction text, newspaper text, academic text の略で，コーパスの4つの主要下位区分を表している（Biber et al., xxvi）。また，†はその用例の一部分を切り詰めていることを意味し，太字部分は注意を引くために強調された主要アイテムであることをそれぞれ意味している（Biber et al., xxvii）。

activity verbs は意志を伴う動作や出来事を主に示すため，動作主の働きをする主語を必要とするものである（Biber et al., 1999, pp.361-362）。activity verbs の例として *bring, buy, carry, come, give, go, leave, move, open, run, take, work* が挙げられている。(10)以降の例文に見られるように activity verbs の中には意志を伴う活動に加えて，意志を伴わない行動や出来事，もしくは静的な関係を表すために使用可能な動詞もある。

(1) *Then you should* **move** *any obstacles before.* (CONV)
(2) *He* **bought** *biscuits and condensed milk.* (FICT)
(3) *The airline had* **opened** *the route on the basis that it would be the first of many.* (NEWS)
(4) *For two years he had* **carried** *a chalice around with him.* (FICT)
(5) *In many of these jobs, women are* **working** *with women only.* (ACAD)
(6) *Well* **give** *it to the dogs, they'll eat it.* (CONV)
(7) *Even the smallest boys* **brought** *little pieces of wood and threw them in.* (FICT †)
(8) *They* **ran**, *on rubbery legs, through an open gate.* (FICT †)
(9) *From Haworth they* **went** *to Holyhead and on to Dublin.* (NEWS)
(10) *New laws resulting from the Children Act* **carry** *a wide range of implications for voluntary groups.* (NEWS †)
(11) *During that time continents, oceans, and mountain chains have* **moved** *horizontally and vertically.* (ACAD †)

(12) *This will **give** the election the chance to get over the hump.* (ACAD †)

(13) *Compulsory elementary education was **working** with a vengeance.* (ACAD)

communication verbsは，スピーキングやライティングなどのコミュニケーション活動を含むactivity verbsの特別な下位範疇と考えられる（Biber et al., 1999, pp.361-362）。この動詞には，*ask, announce, call, discuss, explain, say, shout, speak, state, suggest, talk, tell, write*などが含まれる。

(14) *You **said** you didn't have it.* (CONV)

(15) *I **told** him he was a pain.* (CONV)

(16) *"Stop that", he **shouted**.* (FICT)

(17) *The old man, however, never **spoke** directly to him.* (FICT)

(18) *The organiser **asked** me if I wanted to see how the money was spent.* (NEWS)

(19) *He might find it impossible to **write** in the tone or theme he first took up.* (ACAD †)

またmental verbsは，肉体的な動作を含まず，意志を伴う必要はないが，人間が経験する幅広い活動や状態を示すもので，この動詞の主語には受容者の役割をするものが来ることが多い（Biber et al., 1999, p.362）。この動詞には，知的意味（*think, know*など）と様々な態度や願望を含意する感情的意味（*love, want*など）の両方が知覚（*see, taste*など）やコミュニケーションの受容（*read, hear*など）と共に含まれている。(24)から(27)の例文に見られるように，mental verbsの中には意味において比較的動的な認知活動を表すものも多い。また，(28)以降の例文に見られるように，意味において，より状態を表すものもある。それらの動詞には感情的な状態や態度に関する状態を表す動詞（*enjoy, fear, feel, hate, like, love, prefer, suspect,* *want* など）と同様に，認知的状態を表すもの（*believe, doubt, know, remember, understand* など）が含まれている。

(20) *I **think** it was Freddie Kruger.* (CONV)

(21) *I would **love** to kick it.* (CONV)

(22) *He did not **know** what he expected.* (FICT)

(23) *I **wanted** very much to give him my orange but held back.* (FICT)

(24) *Mr Tench **examined** his companion again with surprise.* (FICT)

(25) *Curry has **decided** to by-pass the Italian Open to lend his support to the Senate Open.* (NEWS †)

(26) *We might even **discover** that he uses a lower number of abstract nouns than other writers of his time.* (ACAD)

(27) *Tillyard (1918b) has **studied** the hairs occurring on the wings of the most primitive groups of Holometabola.* (ACAD)

(28) *Oh yeah, right we all **believe** that.* (CONV)

(29) *Somehow I **doubt** it.* (FICT)

(30) *I **remember** the way you used to bash that ball.* (FICT)

(31) *I **feel** sorry for her.* (CONV)

(32) *He **hated** this weekly ritual of bathing.* (FICT †)

(33) *I **preferred** life as it was.* (NEWS)

causative verbs（*allow, cause, enable, force, help, let, require, permit* など）は，人間や無生物の存在物が，新しい状態を引き起こすことを示すものである（Biber et al., 1999, p.363）。これらの動詞は名詞化された直接目的語や補語節と共起することが多い。

(34) *Still other rules **cause** the deletion of elements from the structure.* (ACAD)

(35) *This information* **enables** *the formulation of precise questions.* (ACAD †)

(36) *The I.U.P.A.C. system* **permits** *the naming of any alkane on sight.* (ACAD †)

(37) *Suction methods for obtaining solution* **require** *careful interpretation.* (ACAD †)

(38) *What* **caused** *you to be ill?* (FICT)

(39) *This would* **help** *protect Jaguar from fluctuations in the dollar.* (NEWS †)

(40) *Police and council leaders agreed to* **let** *a court decide the fate of the trees.* (NEWS †)

(41) *This law* **enables** *the volume of a gas to be calculated.* (ACAD †)

(42) *The second dimension of interpretation then* **requires** *him to judge which of these readings makes the work in progress best.* (ACAD)

verbs of simple occurrenceは，主に意志的な活動以外の出来事（特に物理的な出来事）を伝えるものであり，この動詞の主語は意味的に影響を受ける役割を果たすことが多い（Biber et al., 1999, p.364）。この動詞には*become, change, happen, develop, grow, increase, occur*などがある。

(43) *The lights* **changed.** (CONV)

(44) *The word of adults had once again* **become** *law.* (FICT †)

(45) *Resistant organisms may* **develop** *in the alimentary tract.* (ACAD †)

(46) *The term "feature" has* **occurred** *many times in this chapter.* (ACAD)

verbs of existence or relationshipは，存在物間に存在する状態を示すものである。この動詞で最も良く知られているものは連結動詞（*be, seem, appear*など）で，このような連結動詞は特に主語補語を伴い連結の機能を果たす

ため，主語補語が主語を直接特徴付ける．連結動詞以外でこの動詞に属するものには，例文(49)から(51)のように存在物の特定の状態を示すもの (*exist, live, stay*など) や，(52)から(55)の例文のように存在物間の特定の関係を示すもの (*contain, include, involve, represent*など) がある (Biber et al., 1999, p.364)．

(47) *The problem **is** most acute in rural areas.* (NEWS)

(48) *All these uses **seem** natural and serviceable.* (ACAD)

(49) *I go and **stay** with them.* (CONV)

(50) *She had gone to **live** there during the summer holidays.* (FICT)

(51) *These varying conditions may **exist** in close proximity.* (ACAD †)

(52) *Well she **has** a day off school.* (CONV)

(53) *The exercise will **include** random stop checks by police, and **involve** special constables and traffic wardens.* (NEWS)

(54) *Comparison with equation (3.3) shows that the area **represents** the work done per unit mass.* (ACAD)

(55) *They **contained** large quantities of nitrogen.* (ACAD †)

aspectual verbs (*begin, continue, finish, keep, start, stop*など) は，その他の出来事や活動の経過段階を表すものである (Biber et al., 1999, p.364)．

(56) *She **kept** running out of the room.* (CONV)

(57) *He couldn't **stop** talking about me.* (CONV †)

(58) *Tears **started** to trickle down his cheeks.* (FICT)

(59) *After another day, he **began** to recover.* (FICT)

(60) *The conventional turboprop will certainly **continue** to dominate the market for smaller aircraft.* (ACAD †)

LGSWEは，"The most common lexical verbs"として，少なくとも1つの使用域（conversation, fiction, news, academic prose）において100万語に300回以上出現する動詞114語をそれぞれの動詞が属する意味領域ごとに分けて列挙している[3]。

また，LGSWEは動詞を5つの統合価パタン（intransitive, monotransitive, ditransitive, complex transitive, copular）にも分類している（Biber et al., 1999, pp.380-381）。以下に各動詞の説明と用例を示す。*[ ]* は文法的な単位の境界を示している（Biber et al., xxvii）。

intransitive verbsはSVパタンに現れ，目的語も補語も必要としないものである（Biber et al., 1999, p.380）。

(1) *[More people <S>][*__came__ *<V>]*. (FICT)

monotransitive verbsは，SVO$_d$パタンにおいて単一の直接目的語を必要とするものである。

(2) *[She <S>][*__carried__ *<V>][a long whippy willow twig <O$_d$>]*. (FICT †)

ditransitive verbsはSVO$_i$O$_d$パタンにおいて目的語となる名詞句を2つ必要とするものである。

(3) *[Fred Unsworth <S>][*__gave__ *<V>][her <O$_i$>][a huge vote of confidence <O$_d$>]*. (NEWS †)

---

[3] *be, have, do* は lexical verbs ではなく，primary verbs に分類されているため，LGSWEのpp.367-369のリストには含まれていない。しかし，同書のpp.382-383では*be*が（*be*）という形でリストに現れ，かつ，表に*be*を含んだ数が示されているため*be*は採用した。*fall* もpp.367-369のリストには出てこないが，*be*と同様の理由で114語に含めた。

64

complex transitive verbsはSVO_d P_oパタンにおいて目的語補語（名詞句もしくは形容詞）あるいはSVO_d Aパタンにおいて副詞句が義務的に後続する直接目的語（名詞句）を伴うものである。

(4) *It was natural to [call <V>][them <O_d>][photons <P_o>]*. (ACAD)
(5) *He reached out to [put <V>][his hand <O_d>][on the child's shoulder <A>]*. (FICT)

copular verbsは，SVP_sパタンにおいて主語補語（名詞，形容詞，前置詞句），あるいはSVAパタンにおいて状況を表す副詞句が義務的に伴うものである。

(6) *[Carrie <S>][felt <V>][a little less bold<P_s>]*. (FICT †)
(7) *I wasn't planning on [staying <V>][at Terry and Lindsey's <A>]*. (CONV †)

表12. Transitive, intransitive, and copular patterns of common verbs, by semantic domain

domain	intransitive only	transitive only	copular only	transitive and intransitive	copular and intransitive	copular and transitive	all three
activity	5	19	0	22	2	0	2
communication	0	6	0	6	0	0	0
mental	0	8	0	14	0	1	0
causative	0	3	0	1	0	0	0
occurrence	3	0	1	2	0	0	1
existence	2	5	2	1	3	0	0
aspectual	0	0	0	4	0	0	1
total	10	41	3	50	5	1	4

表13. 動詞の意味領域および統合価パタン

動詞の意味領域	動詞の統合価パタン
Activity verbs	Intransitive only: *fall, sit, smile, stare, wait*
	Transitive only: *add, bring, buy, carry, catch, give, hold, make, obtain, pick, produce, provide, put, reduce, send, spend, take, use, wear*
	Both intransitive and transitive: *apply, eat, follow, form, leave, lose, meet, move, open, pass, pay, play, reach, run, sell, shake, show, try, walk, watch, win, work*
	Both intransitive and copular: *come, go*
	Transitive, intransitive and copular: *turn, get*
Communication verbs	Transitive only: *describe, claim, offer, suggest, say, thank*
	Both intransitive and transitive: *ask, call, speak, talk, tell, write*
Mental verbs	Transitive only: *assume, determine, expect, find, like, mean, need, want*
	Both intransitive and transitive: *believe, consider, hear, hope, know, listen, love, understand, read, remember, see, suppose, think, wonder*
	Both intransitive and copular: *feel*
Causative verbs	Transitive only: *allow, let, require*
	Both intransitive and transitive: *help*
Occurrence verbs	Intransitive only: *die, happen, occur*
	Both intransitive and transitive: *change, develop*
	Copular only: *become*
	Transitive, intransitive and copular: *grow*
Existence verbs	Intransitive only: *exist, live*
	Transitive only: *contain, include, indicate, involve, represent*
	Both intransitive and transitive: *stand*
	Copular only: *(be), seem*
	Both intransitive and copular: *appear, look, stay*
Aspectual verbs	Both intransitive and transitive: *begin, continue, start, stop*
	Transitive, intransitive and copular: *keep*

LGSWEが挙げる114語の最も一般的な動詞の意味領域と統合価パタンごとの分布，およびその内容をそれぞれ表12，表13に示す（Biber et al., 1999, pp.382-383）。

　表12から明らかなように，意味領域において最も頻繁に使われる動詞は，activity verbsである。また，動詞の統合価パタンにおいては，他動詞と自動詞の両方で使用可能な動詞が最も多いことがわかる。これらの特徴は，後段で日本人英語初学者のための基本動詞リストを提案する際に参照する資料とするものである。

3.3　*Longman Lexicon of Contemporary English*

　Longman Lexicon of Contemporary English（McArthur, 1981）（以下LLCEと略す）は，「分類配列の本体に見出し語の意味・用法の記述を加え，有機的に一体化したthesaurus-dictionaryつまり'lexicon'である」（寺澤，1981, p.3）。LLCEは，約15,000語を実用的一般的特性に基づいた14の意味領域（semantic fields）に分類している：A Life and Living Things［生・生物］；B The Body: its Functions and Welfare［身体の機能・福祉］；C People and the Family［人間・家族］；D Buildings, Houses, the Home, Clothes, Belongings, and Personal Care［建物，家，家庭，衣服］；E Food, Drink, and Farming［飲食物・飼養］；F Feelings, Emotions, Attitudes, and Sensations［感情・感覚］；G Thought and Communication, Language and Grammar［思考・伝達，言語・文法］；H Substances, Materials, Objects, and Equipment［物質，器具，電気，武器］；I Arts and Crafts, Science and Technology, Industry and Education［科学・技術，産業，教育］；J Numbers, Measurement, Money, and Commerce［数，度量衡，金融，商業］；K Entertainment, Sports, and Games［娯楽，スポーツ，ゲーム］；L Space and Time［空間・時間］；M Movement, Location, Travel, and Transport［運

動, 運輸, 場所］; N General and Abstract Terms ［一般・抽象語］)
(McArthur, 1981, v-vi; ［ ］内の日本語訳は寺澤, 1981, p.3)。それゆえ, 動詞も同じ意味領域を構成する類義語ごとにまとめてある。例えばA Life and Living ThingsのA1 *verbs*: existing and causing to existには, *exist, be, create, animate*という順に動詞が挙げられ, それぞれの定義が以下のようにされている。

> A1 *verbs*: existing and causing to exist
> exist ［Wv6; IØ］ to be real; be there in fact: *The world exists and we are part of it. The planet Earth has existed for millions of years. Fairies don't exist in real life, only in stories.*
> be ［Wv6; IØ］ *fml & tech* to exist: *Whatever is, is right. The universe is, but we don't know why.*
> create ［T1］ to cause to exist: *Many people say that God created the world.*
> animate ［T1］ 1 to give life to 2 to make lively or exciting: *Laughter animated his face for a moment.* 3 to cause to become active; interest: *His excitement animated us all.*

LLCEに使用されている定義は, *Longman Dictionary of Contemporary English* (1977) に基づいており (McArthur, 1981, xii; 寺澤, 1981, p.1, p.4), LDOCEの2,000語の定義語が使用されている (McArthur, xii)。それゆえ各見出し語にはLDOCEが使用している動詞のパタン (Wv6, T1など) が付記されている。しかし, 3.1, 3.2で言及したICE-GBやLGSWEとは異なり, LLCEは動詞のパタンよりも, 現実世界における意味の領域を重視している。この情報から, 英語母語話者が頻繁に用いる動詞 (LGSWE) の意味領域がどのように展開するのか, また, 学習指導要領に共通して現れる動詞 (付録2参照) について, 日本人英語初学者のために書かれたFries and

Fries（1961）のコーパス内に現れる動詞（付録3参照）について，さらには，LDOCEの定義語中の動詞（付録4参照）について，意味領域から見た場合の領域間の分布の異同をまとめると次の表のようになる。

表14. 動詞の意味領域の分布（百分率と度数の併記）

	A	B	C	D	E	F	G	H	I	J	K	L	M	N	該当無し
LDOCE	1.0%	0.3%	3.9%	8.3%	1.6%	10.9%	18.6%	2.2%	3.9%	4.8%	2.2%	3.2%	14.4%	23.1%	1.6%
(n = 312)	(3)	(1)	(12)	(26)	(5)	(34)	(58)	(7)	(12)	(15)	(7)	(10)	(45)	(72)	(5)
LGSWE	1.7%	0%	2.5%	9.1%	0.8%	13.2%	18.2%	1.7%	5.0%	5.0%	2.5%	4.1%	14.9%	21.5%	0%
(n = 121)	(2)	(0)	(3)	(11)	(1)	(16)	(22)	(2)	(6)	(6)	(3)	(5)	(18)	(26)	(0)
学習指導要領	0%	1.2%	1.2%	9.3%	2.3%	14.0%	20.9%	0%	4.7%	4.7%	4.7%	3.5%	19.8%	14.0%	0%
(n = 86)	(0)	(1)	(1)	(8)	(2)	(12)	(18)	(0)	(4)	(4)	(4)	(3)	(17)	(12)	(0)
Fries and Fries	0.6%	1.7%	1.7%	9.1%	4.0%	8.6%	20.6%	1.7%	3.4%	8.6%	3.4%	1.7%	17.7%	16.6%	0.6%
(n = 175)	(1)	(3)	(3)	(16)	(7)	(15)	(36)	(3)	(6)	(15)	(6)	(3)	(31)	(29)	(1)

Note: A Life and Living Things; B The Body: its Functions and Welfare; C People and the Family; D Buildings, Houses, the Home, Clothes, Belongings, and Personal Care; E Food, Drink, and Farming; F Feelings, Emotions, Attitudes, and Sensations; G Thought and Communication, Language and Grammar; H Substances, Materials, Objects, and Equipment; I Arts and Crafts, Science and Technology, Industry and Education; J Numbers, Measurement, Money, and Commerce; K Entertainment, Sports, and Games; L Space and Time; M Movement, Location, Travel, and Transport; N General and Abstract Terms (McArthur, 1981, v-vi)

1つの語が複数の意味領域に現れることから，合計した数が語形のみの数よりも多い。この結果を百分率で比較すると，以下の図のようになる。

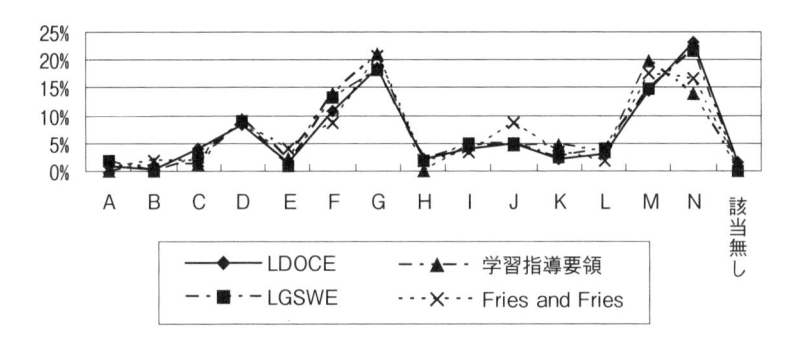

図8．4つの資料における動詞の意味領域ごとの分布

4つの資料の動詞の意味領域において，5％以上差があるのがF（Feelings, Emotions, Attitudes, and Sensations）の学習指導要領（14.0%）とFries and Fries（8.6%），M（Movement, Location, Travel, and Transport）のLDOCE（14.4%）と学習指導要領（19.8%），N（General and Abstract Terms）のLDOCE（23.1%）と学習指導要領（14.0%）である。このように資料間において若干のばらつきが見られるが，どの資料もほぼ同じグラフを描いていることは注目に値する。

大きなピークを示しているのはG（Thought and Communication, Language and Grammar）とN（General and Abstract Terms）である。逆にゼロに近い値を示すのは，B（The Body: its Functions and Welfare），E（Food, Drink, and Farming），H（Substances, Materials, Objects, and Equipment）である。

名詞や形容詞をこのスケールに当てはめれば，おそらく異なる結果が出るだろう。動詞の基本的な機能は，「論題（Arguments）をつなぐ」ことであるので，GやNが多くなるのは頷ける。このグラフを第5章で提案する基本動詞に当てはめた際に同様な分布を示すかどうかを検証する必要があ

る。

　3.1，3.2，3.3で見てきたように，動詞にはいくつかの異なる捉え方がある。これらは，これまでの語形の出現頻度や使用領域に基づいた語彙選定の方法では欠けていた概念のように思われる。学習者に受容語彙として，それもその語というよりその語の語形を「見たことがある」という程度の学習をさせることを目標とするのであれば，語形の出現頻度などで語彙選定をしても事足りるだろう。しかし「誰」が「何」を行ったのか，正しく理解したり表したりするためには，言い換えれば，英語の基本構造を学習するという観点からは，上で言及してきたように3つの動詞の捉え方をかけ合わせて語の選定を行うことが必要となる。

第4章　外国語としての英語の学習と語彙に関する調査

　本章では，日本の外国語としての英語の学習における語彙の扱いについて論じるために，過去の学習指導要領における必修語中の動詞の変遷を概観する。本章で扱う学習指導要領は，『中学校学習指導要領（昭和33年10月1日 文部省告示第81号）』，『中学校学習指導要領（昭和44年4月14日 文部省告示第199号）』，『中学校学習指導要領（昭和52年7月23日 文部省告示第156号）』，『中学校学習指導要領（平成元年3月15日 文部省告示第25号）』である。これらの学習指導要領の別表に挙げられた必修語における動詞の数と割合，および具体的な内容，さらにclause typeと意味領域（semantic domain）を調査する。また，調査した4つの学習指導要領の別表に共通して挙げられてきた動詞にも焦点を当てる。なお，『中学校・高等学校学習指導要領 外国語科英語編〔試案〕（昭和27年3月20日 文部省発行）』には具体的な語彙リストの記載が無いため，また『中学校学習指導要領（平成10年12月14日 文部省告示第176号）』には，語彙リストの記載が機能語を中心とする100語のみとなり，さらに平成20年告示のものからは語彙リストの記載が無くなったため，この調査の対象とはしていない。

4.1　調査資料

　昭和33年から平成元年までに文部省が告示した4つの学習指導要領の別表に挙げられた必修語を調査資料とした（昭和33年から昭和52年までに告示されたものは大村他［1980］を参照，平成元年告示のものは文部省［1989］を参照した）。

4.2 調査対象

4.2.1 必修語とその中の動詞の数および割合

　学習指導要領の別表に挙げられた必修語と，その中の動詞の数，および必修語に占める動詞の割合を検証する。いずれの学習指導要領の必修語にも品詞の表記が無いため，文部省（1959, 1970, 1978, 1989）に従い，言語材料の「動作などを表すもの」に挙げられた語を動詞として扱う。
　また，必修語として基本形（もしくは原形）とその異形（*a, an; do, does, did; better, best; child, children* など）が別語として扱われているが，そのような基本形と異形が，異なった告示年度の学習指導要領に独立して現れているため，動詞の数を数える際にはそれらを原形にまとめることはしていない。

4.2.2 学習指導要領の動詞の clause type

　告示年度別の学習指導要領の動詞と，4つの学習指導要領に共通して現れる動詞をそれぞれICE-GBのclause typeに従って分類し，4つの学習指導要領に共通して現れる動詞のclause typeをICE-GBの動詞のclause typeと比較した。4つの学習指導要領に共通する動詞のclause typeをICE-GBのclause typeと比較するのは，これまでに日本人英語初学者に提示され続けてきた動詞の特徴を明らかにするためである。
　上述の通り，学習指導要領の必修語の中には動詞の基本形と異形（*am, are, be, is; has, have* など）が含まれているが，clause typeの調査を行うため，ここでは動詞の異形は全て原形にまとめた。

4.2.3 学習指導要領の動詞の意味領域

　告示年度別の学習指導要領の動詞と，4つの学習指導要領に共通して現れる動詞をそれぞれLGSWEの挙げる意味領域（semantic domain）ごとに

分類し，4つの学習指導要領に共通して現れる動詞の意味領域とLGSWE に掲載された114語の動詞の意味領域と比較した。4つの学習指導要領の動詞の意味領域とLGSWEの動詞の意味領域を比較した理由は，4.2.2に挙げた理由と同様である。

4.3 調査結果

4.3.1 必修語とその中の動詞の数および割合

学習指導要領の別表に挙げられた必修語の数とその中の動詞の数，および必修語に占める動詞の割合は表15の通りである。

表15. 必修語とその中の動詞の数，および割合

	必修語	動詞	動詞の割合
昭和33年告示	520	96	18.5%
昭和44年告示	610	116	19.0%
昭和52年告示	490	100	20.4%
平成元年告示	507	106	20.9%

動詞の割合は告示年度によって多少の差があるものの，いずれも20％程度であり，特に偏りは無いように思われる。上述の通り，表15に挙げた必修語および動詞の数は基本形と異形を含んだ数であり，動詞の割合もそれに従った割合であるため，必修語と動詞，それぞれに出てくる異形を基本形にまとめて語数をカウントすると，この結果とは若干の誤差が生じることが予想される。

さらに，増減した必修語の数とその中の動詞の数，ならびに増減した必修語の中の動詞の割合を表16に示した。

表16. 増減した必修語の数とその中の動詞の数，および動詞の割合

	必修語 増加	必修語 減少	必修語内の動詞 増加	必修語内の動詞 減少	必修語内の動詞の割合 増加	必修語内の動詞の割合 減少
昭和33年告示	—	—	—	—	—	—
昭和44年告示	98	8	20	0	20.4%	0%
昭和52年告示	6	126	2	18	33.3%	14.3%
平成元年告示	30	13	7	1	23.3%	7.7%

増減した必修語内の増加した動詞と減少した動詞のそれぞれの割合は，告示年度によって大きく異なっており，それぞれの学習指導要領の動詞の増加と減少の間にも大差が認められる。

4.3.2 学習指導要領の動詞の clause type

告示年度別の学習指導要領の動詞の clause type の分布は表17の通りである。

表17. 告示年度別学習指導要領の動詞の clause type（百分率と度数の併記）

	intr	cop	montr	dimontr	ditr	cxtr	trans
昭和33年告示	30.0%	5.5%	27.9%	3.1%	7.9%	14.8%	10.7%
($n = 290$)	(87)	(16)	(81)	(9)	(23)	(43)	(31)
昭和44年告示	30.9%	5.8%	28.3%	2.6%	7.8%	14.7%	9.8%
($n = 346$)	(107)	(20)	(98)	(9)	(27)	(51)	(34)
昭和52年告示	29.6%	5.7%	28.3%	2.9%	8.3%	15.0%	10.2%
($n = 314$)	(93)	(18)	(89)	(9)	(26)	(47)	(32)
平成元年告示	29.4%	5.8%	28.8%	2.7%	7.6%	15.2%	10.6%
($n = 330$)	(97)	(19)	(95)	(9)	(25)	(50)	(35)

1つの動詞が複数の clause type で使用されるため，それらを合計すると，表15に示した年度別の学習指導要領の動詞の数よりも動詞の数が大幅に

増えている。この結果を百分率で比較すると，以下の図9のようになる。

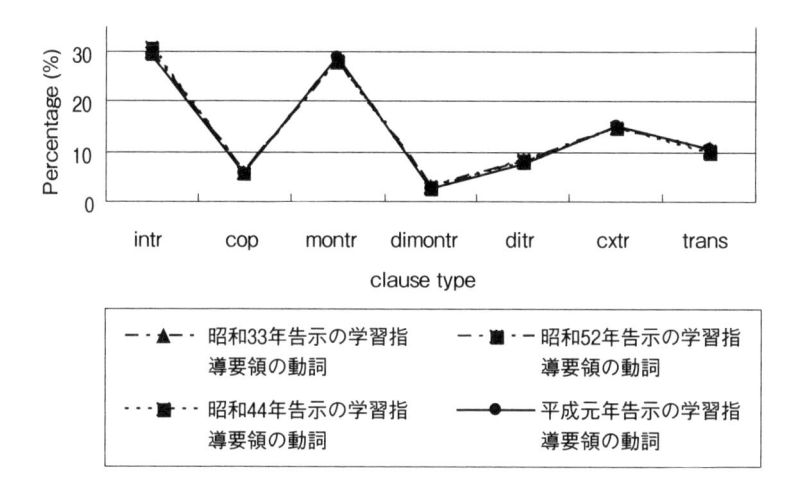

図9．告示年度別学習指導要領の動詞のclause typeの比率の比較

図9では，4つの学習指導要領の動詞のclause typeの割合を表す線が1本の線のように重なっており，告示年度が異なっていても，調査した4つの学習指導要領の動詞のclause typeの割合がほぼ同じであることを示している。また，学習指導要領の動詞のclause typeでは，intransitiveとmonotransitiveの割合が高く，complex-transitive, transitive, ditransitiveがそれに続き，copular, dimonotransitiveが比較的に少ないということが明らかになった。

次に，4つの学習指導要領に共通する動詞のclause typeとICE-GBの動詞のclause typeの分布を表18に示した。

表18. ICE-GBと4つの学習指導要領に共通する動詞のclause type
（百分率と度数の併記）

	intr	cop	montr	dimontr	ditr	cxtr	trans
ICE-GB	33.1%	1.2%	53.3%	0.5%	1.7%	7.2%	3.1%
($n = 5,167$)	(1,710)	(61)	(2,752)	(24)	(87)	(371)	(162)
学習指導要領	29.0%	5.3%	27.8%	3.4%	8.3%	15.4%	10.9%
($n = 266$)	(77)	(14)	(74)	(9)	(22)	(41)	(29)

この結果を百分率で比較すると，図10のようになる。

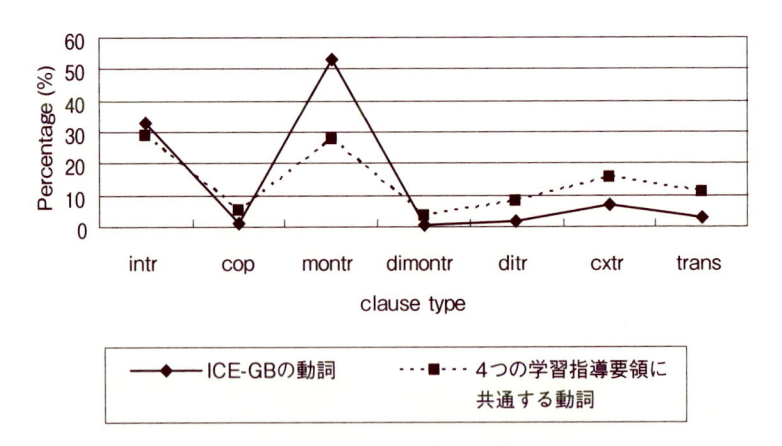

図10. ICE-GBと4つの学習指導要領に共通する動詞のclause typeの比率の比較

4つの学習指導要領に共通する動詞のclause typeでは，intransitiveとmonotransitiveがほぼ同様の割合で最も高いのに対し，ICE-GBの動詞のclause typeではmonotransitiveの割合がその他のclause typeに大差をつけて高い割合を示している。

ICE-GBの動詞のclause typeと4つの学習指導要領に共通する動詞のclause typeの差をSPSSによるχ二乗検定により検討した結果，$\chi^2(6, N = 5,433) = 219.57, p < .01$であり，両者の間には有意な差が認められた。次

にmonotransitiveとそれ以外のclause typeに分けてχ二乗検定を行ったところ，$\chi^2(1, N = 5,433) = 65.60, p < .01$であり，両者の間に有意な差が認められた。この結果により，monotransitiveの配分が学習指導要領ではICE-GBに比べて少ないことが明らかとなった。

4.3.3 学習指導要領の動詞の意味領域

告示年度別の学習指導要領の動詞の意味領域の分布は表19の通りである。

表19. 告示年度別学習指導要領の動詞の意味領域（百分率と度数の併記）

意味領域	昭和33年告示	昭和44年告示	昭和52年告示	平成元年告示
activity	48.9%（43）	55.6%（60）	51.0%（49）	47.1%（48）
communication	14.8%（13）	12.0%（13）	14.6%（14）	15.7%（16）
mental	18.2%（16）	15.7%（17）	16.7%（16）	20.6%（21）
causative	2.3%（2）	1.9%（2）	2.1%（2）	2.0%（2）
occurrence	4.6%（4）	3.7%（4）	3.1%（3）	3.0%（3）
existence	5.7%（5）	5.6%（6）	6.3%（6）	5.9%（6）
aspectual	5.7%（5）	5.6%（6）	6.3%（6）	5.9%（6）
合　　計	88	108	96	102

合計数が表15で挙げた動詞の数よりも少ないのは，告示年度別の学習指導要領の動詞の中に動詞の基本形と異形（*am, are, be, been, is, was, were; had, has, have*）が含まれているためである。この結果を百分率で比較すると，図11のようになる。

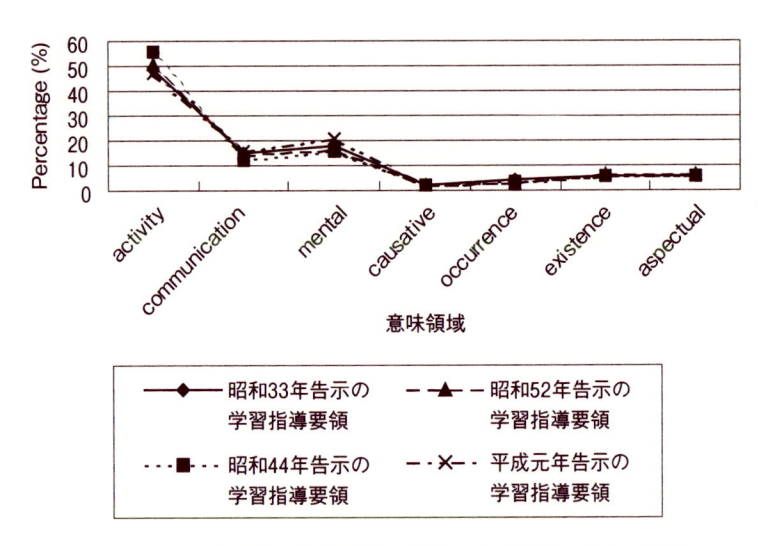

図11. 告示年度別学習指導要領の動詞の意味領域の比率の比較

図8で示したclause typeの割合と比較すると若干のずれが見られるが、告示年度別の4つの学習指導要領の動詞の意味領域の割合もほぼ同じであると言える。

次に4つの学習指導要領に共通する80語の動詞をLGSWEの動詞の意味領域に従って分類した結果をLGSWEの114語の動詞の分布と共に表20に示す。

表20. LGSWEと4つの学習指導要領に共通する動詞の意味領域
　　　（百分率と度数の併記）

意味領域	LGSWEの動詞	学習指導要領に共通する80語の動詞
activity	43.86％ （50）	46.25％ （37）
communication	10.53％ （12）	16.25％ （13）
mental	20.18％ （23）	18.75％ （15）
causative	3.51％ （4）	2.50％ （2）

occurrence	6.14％　（7）	3.75％　（3）
existence	11.40％　（13）	6.25％　（5）
aspectual	4.39％　（5）	6.25％　（5）

この結果を百分率で比較すると，図12のようになる。

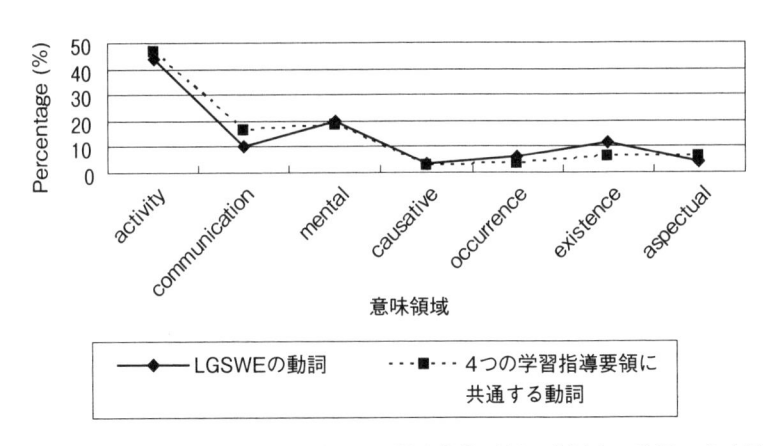

図12. LGSWEの動詞の意味領域と4つの学習指導要領に共通する動詞の意味領域の比率の比較

LGSWEの動詞の意味領域と学習指導要領に共通する動詞の意味領域の割合は，いずれもactivityが最も高く，mentalがそれに続き，その他の意味領域はほぼ横並びである。LGSWEと4つの学習指導要領に共通する動詞の意味領域の差をSPSSによるχ二乗検定により検討した結果でも，両者の間には有意な差が認められなかった。

4.4　考察

4.4.1　必修語とその中の動詞の数および割合について

必修語に占める動詞の割合は，いずれの学習指導要領でも20％程度であ

る。しかし，改訂に伴って増減した必修語とその中の動詞の増減数にはばらつきが見られ，割合においても一定ではない。これは，語彙選定の際に品詞（本書で明らかになったものは動詞）の割合が考慮されていないということを窺わせる。

4.4.2 学習指導要領の動詞のclause typeについて

　告示年度別の学習指導要領の動詞のclause typeを比較した結果，4つの学習指導要領が重なりを見せているということが明らかになった。この結果から，改訂に伴って語彙の変化を多少伴ってはいてもclause typeに関しては，大きく変化が生じていないということが窺える。また，ICE-GBの動詞のclause typeと4つの学習指導要領に共通する動詞のclause typeの間に有意差が認められたことによって，これまで学習者に提示されてきたものが自然な英語の動詞のclause typeの割合とは異なっていたということを意味している。勿論，英語母語話者によって高頻度で使用されている語彙をそのまま教授することが日本人英語初学者にとって最も有用だとは必ずしも言うことはできない。むしろ英語母語話者にはあまり使用されない語でも，英語学習に必要であれば，それらを採用する必要があると考えられる。しかし，英語の持つclause typeの割合は英語学習にそのまま取り入れることは可能である。重要なのは，その割合に合わせてどのような語彙を選定するかである。ここではclause typeの割合の多さと学習者への提示回数の多さは同じではないことに注意が必要である。いずれのclause typeも満遍なく学習者に習得させる必要があるため，出現頻度の高いclause typeでは，そのclause typeで使用可能な動詞の種類を多くして教授し，出現頻度の低いclause typeではそのclause typeで使用可能な動詞の種類を少なくして，そのclause typeを扱う回数を増やすなどの方法が考えられる。

4.4.3 学習指導要領の動詞の意味領域について

　告示年度別の学習指導要領の動詞の意味領域の分布を見ると，それぞれ

の学習指導要領の動詞の使用される意味領域にはあまり違いが見られないということが明らかになった。

また，4つの学習指導要領に共通する動詞の意味領域とLGSWEの動詞の意味領域の分布間に有意差が無かったことに関しては，LGSWEが1つの動詞にその動詞の持つ最も一般的な意味領域のみを（全てではないがほとんどの場合）付していることから（Biber et al., 1999, p.361），学習指導要領に挙げられた動詞も，それと同じ使い方をすることを前提とした場合に，学習指導要領に挙げられた動詞が英語母語話者の使用する自然な動詞の使い方を再現することが可能であるということを示したに過ぎない。

いずれにせよ，4つの学習指導要領に共通する動詞とLGSWEに挙げられた動詞の意味領域が同様のものであることから，学習指導要領の動詞のmonotransitiveの割合をICE-GBのmonotransitiveの割合と同様に配列すれば，よりオーセンティックなものに近い自然な英語を学習者に提示することができると考えられる。

第5章　日本人英語初学者のための
　　　　基本動詞リスト

　外国語としての英語の学習にとって，最も基本とすべきは，英語の構造の習得であると考えられる。この考え方に立てば，英語の基本構造を決定する要因として最も影響力を発揮するのは動詞の型，clause typeであると言うことができる。

　学習用の材料として，学習者をどこへ向かわせるか，そのターゲットは，英語母語話者が内在化している英語の構造である必要がある。それゆえ，第4章では英語母語話者のオーセンティックな言語材料としてICE-GBを用いて，そのclause typeの在り方を求めた。日本人英語初学者が使う教材においても，基本的にはこのclause typeの在り方は英語母語話者のそれと相似形であることが必要となる。なぜならば，外国語としての英語の学習者が習得しなければならない英語は，英語母語話者の英語と質的には相似形のものでなければ，習得後において英語母語話者の英語との相互互換性を欠くことになるからである。もし互換性を欠くならば，「通じない英語」を操作しなければならないことに陥る。これでは，学習の目的は達成することができない。

　日本人英語初学者にとって必要なのは，英語母語話者の使用する英語の持つclause typeと相似形でありながら，量的にはそれより遥かに少ない語彙数で，学習の発展性を見込むことができるものである。

　第2章で，これまでに開発されてきた「語彙リスト」を概観し，いずれのリストも「語形を中心とする頻度」をほぼ唯一の尺度としてでき上がっていることを明らかにした。また，その後開発されている語彙リスト（竹蓋・中條，JACET 8000など）は，英語を実際に使って学業を進めたり，種々

の職業に就いたりする際に「必要とされるであろう語彙」をそれと同じ世界で生活している英語母語話者の使っている語彙を目的に沿ったコーパスから取り出して、頻度順に並べたものである。再度繰り返すが、「語形を中心とする頻度」に頼る語彙の選択では、日本人英語初学者にとって、基本となる英語の構造を学習させるための適切な語彙を得ることはできない。

これらをもとに、実際の英語使用のジャンルや使用域に拘束されず、いかなるジャンルや使用域で将来英語を使うにしても、その基礎を養うこととなる「基本」の部分を取り出して、適切な語彙リストを日本人英語初学者のための教材を作成する原資料としなければならない。

外国人英語学習者のために編まれた英英辞書の中で、全ての説明を2,000語レベルで収めているLDOCEは、基本動詞を選択するのに最も相応しい素材を提供してくれると考えられる。それゆえ日本人英語初学者が学習する基本的な動詞はまず、この中に含まれていると考えられる。

日本人英語初学者が学習すべき動詞の数は、全学習語彙の約20%と考えられる。なぜならば自然なコーパスの中での動詞が占める割合は約20%なのである（Dogishi, 2006）。

筆者が考察を進めている日本人英語初学者のための英語の基本動詞リストは、我が国の英語教育をベースとしているので、平成24年から施行される学習指導要領に基づく英語学習に反映されることが必要である。新学習指導要領では、学習すべき語彙の数は1,200語程度としてある。従って、この語彙の中に占める動詞の割合は240語程度となるべきである。

この240語程度を得る工程は次の通りである。まず、LDOCEの定義語について整理する。LDOCEの定義語の中から動詞を抜き出す。第2章で言及した通り、LDOCEの定義語（2,065語）には品詞のラベル付けが徹底されていないため、筆者は次のものを動詞として捉えた：LDOCEの見出し語に動詞として挙がっているもの595語のうち、話し言葉（S）と書き言葉（W）の出現頻度が高いもの（S1W1, S1W2, S1W3, S2W1, S2W2, S3W1, S1,

W1）286語（付録4参照）。S2とはその語が話し言葉において最も出現頻度の高い2,000語のうちの1つであることを表している（Summers et al., 2003, xiv）。筆者は上位2,000語までのものを中心に学習者用の基本動詞のベースとすることを考えたが，S1W3のように，片方が上位1,000語である場合は動詞とみなした。しかしながら，話し言葉と書き言葉のいずれか一方のみが出現頻度が高い場合，偏りを考慮して上位1,000語以内のもののみ（S1，W1）を採用し，S2，S3，W2，W3は除いた。そして，それらの動詞をLDOCEに挙げられた1番目の語義で使用されるclause typeに分類し，ICE-GBに振り分けた。

これに，英語で最も一般的なものとして挙げられたLGSWEの114語の動詞（第3章P.66参照）を重ね，原資料とした。そして，日本人英語初学者にとって有用な教育語彙がどのように現れるかを見るため，原資料のリストに学習指導要領の動詞80語（付録2参照）と，Fries and Fries（1961）の動詞166語（付録3参照）を重ね合わせた。この結果，原資料と教育語彙のほとんどが重なりを見せていることが明らかになった。

第4章に示したICE-GBの挙げるclause typeごとの動詞の割合に従って240語の動詞のclause typeごとの動詞の数を求め，ICE-GBと原資料の重なり部分で頻度の高い順に上から動詞を選択していく。その際，原資料と重なるものを優先させるため，LDOCEの定義動詞との重なりを示さない以下の動詞は基本動詞のリストに含めないこととした。

1）学習指導要領とFries and Friesに重なる動詞
2）学習指導要領のみに出てくる動詞
3）Fries and Friesのみに出てくる動詞

このような手順を経て得られた動詞を用いることで，英語の基本構造の学習は過不足なくできると考えられる。

以下に上記の方法で得られた実際の語彙リストを示す。各語の左側の数

字は通し番号を表し，右側の数値はICE-GBにおけるその語の出現頻度を表している。網掛け部分はLDOCE，LGSWEとFries and Fries (1961) の動詞との重なりを示している。

表21．日本人英語初学者のための基本動詞の提案

Intransitive

1	go	2,567	28	change	134	55	stop	67
2	come	1,838	29	exist	134	56	end	64
3	say	1,400	30	hear	134	57	develop	62
4	look	890	31	grow	128	58	hang	59
5	work	639	32	arrive	124	59	help	59
6	know	620	33	agree	121	60	read	59
7	happen	521	34	listen	119	61	report	59
8	talk	472	35	begin	117	62	worry	56
9	live	367	36	play	112	63	drive	55
10	move	307	37	lie 1	110	64	fight	48
11	speak	281	38	rise	99	65	win	47
12	run	251	39	ask	96	66	finish	46
13	write	248	40	pay	91	67	close	45
14	start	244	41	act	85	68	fly	42
15	sit	239	42	break	85	69	fit	41
16	occur	231	43	suffer	85	70	ring	41
17	stand	185	44	continue	84	71	hope	40
18	turn	181	45	leave	84	72	care	38
19	lead	179	46	increase	81	73	learn	38
20	wait	170	47	return	81	74	sing	38
21	try	164	48	follow	78	75	eat	37
22	stay	155	49	matter	78	76	explain	36
23	walk	153	50	remember	75	77	sleep	36
24	depend	150	51	meet	73	78	argue	34
25	fall	148	52	travel	72	79	decide	34
26	die	144	53	call	67			
27	apply	135	54	pass	67			

Copular

1	be	29,179
2	become	570
3	feel	273

Monotransitive

1	have	3,967
2	do	2,568
3	think	2,322
4	say	1,965
5	get	1,927
6	see	1,462
7	take	1,434
8	know	1,377
9	make	1,225
10	use	1,162
11	want	1,104
12	find	633
13	mean	613
14	try	589
15	give	562
16	like	486
17	show	468
18	need	406
19	bring	365
20	provide	365
21	leave	354
22	write	327
23	produce	324
24	pay	310
25	believe	303
26	play	292
27	hear	281
28	remember	278
29	hope	271
30	feel	266

31	read	265
32	involve	237
33	suggest	237
34	meet	234
35	hold	231
36	send	230
37	include	228
38	decide	227
39	carry	222
40	set	221
41	understand	209
42	receive	208
43	require	206
44	buy	200
45	lose	199
46	cause	194
47	consider	191
48	help	184
49	mention	183
50	achieve	181
51	follow	178
52	reach	178
53	change	176
54	spend	175
55	develop	168
56	accept	167
57	describe	164
58	win	164
59	learn	162
60	build	155

61	agree	153
62	expect	153
63	ask	151
64	pick	151
65	reduce	151
66	add	148
67	affect	140
68	realize	139
69	cover	138
70	increase	138
71	offer	138
72	enjoy	137
73	explain	135
74	support	135
75	suppose	135
76	base	133
77	discuss	133
78	wish	133
79	face	131
80	raise	131
81	represent	131
82	cut	129
83	wear	124
84	claim	122
85	establish	119
86	draw	118
87	contain	117
88	kill	115
89	choose	114
90	pass	114

91	thank	114
92	sell	113
93	remove	112
94	forget	111
95	manage	111
96	love	109
97	hit	108
98	introduce	108
99	measure	108
100	avoid	106
101	form	103
102	join	101
103	recognize	100

104	call	98
105	indicate	98
106	miss	97
107	tell	95
108	start	92
109	control	90
110	turn	90
111	check	89
112	design	86
113	notice	86
114	catch	83
115	replace	83
116	destroy	82

117	open	82
118	express	80
119	compare	79
120	report	79
121	improve	78
122	watch	78
123	admit	77
124	break	77
125	protect	77
126	save	77
127	determine	76
128	complete	75

Dimonotransitive

1	tell	155

Ditransitive

1	give	560
2	tell	484

3	ask	91
4	show	82

Complex-transitive

1	put	390
2	keep	213
3	find	205
4	leave	112
5	describe	91
6	regard	82

7	bring	81
8	place	74
9	use	44
10	think	33
11	send	29
12	treat	24

13	name	20
14	push	15
15	force	12
16	like	8
17	pull	7

Transitive

1	allow	217
2	let	192
3	see	170

4	want	134
5	expect	97
6	hear	61

7	help	61

おわりに

　日本における外国語としての英語教育のシラバス中に記載される言語材料のうち，総量としての1,200語程度ということ以外は語彙についての記載が平成20年告示の学習指導要領から消えた。平成10年告示の学習指導要領においても必修語として示されたのは，あえて選定する必要のない機能語100語のみで，全体としては900語を教えるようにとの記載だけであった。それまでの学習指導要領は昭和33年告示以来，必修語の語彙リストを載せていた。

　日本の学校教育において使用される教科用図書のベースとなっているシラバスは，「文法シラバス」に区分されるタイプのものと考えられるが，それならば，言語材料は明示されなければならない。それにも関わらず，「語彙」に関しては数のみで，あとは教材作成者に任せるということに大いに違和感を覚える。

　これがこの研究の発端であった。これまでに提案されてきた語彙リストについて調べ，その性質は把握できた。結局は，「語形の出現頻度」がほぼ唯一の選定基準となっていることが明らかとなった。歴史上著名なMichael WestのGSLをはじめ，現代においてもなお提案され続けている語彙リストは，やはり，語形の頻度を頼りに選定されていると言える。英語学習者が将来どのような職業に就くか，また英語をどのように使うかによって，必要とされる語彙が様々に異なってくるのは当然であり，いわゆる，ESP（English for Specific Purposes）のコンテクストでは極めて自然である。しかし，筆者には，日本人英語初学者が英語を学習し始める時に「必要な語彙」が設定されていてしかるべきであるという考えが根底にある。

　本書では，外国語学習のためのコーパスがあるとすると，コーパス中の異語のうち，動詞が占める割合は約20％であることをいくつかのコーパス

から検証した。また，英語の学習にとって重要なウエイトを占める英語の構造の学習については，動詞のclause typeが最も重要なカギを握っていることも確認した。現在，英語のコーパスは数多く存在するが，「文法的タグ付き」のコーパスは，ICE-GBがその代表であると言うことができる。従って，このコーパスから，英語のclause typeごとの動詞の実態を引き出し，一般に外国人英語学習者用の辞書として広く使用されているLDOCEの定義語をこのclause typeにより分類し，clause typeごとの基本的な定義語として使われている動詞の実態を取り出した。また，英語母語話者が最も頻繁に用いる動詞をLGSWEから取り出し，それをICE-GBのclause typeによって分類し，代表的な英語の構造を作り出すことができる動詞の在り方，分布を取り出した。

　また，日本人中学生のために特別に作られたFries and Fries（1961）という大変貴重なコーパスの中から動詞を取り出して，上記の動詞群と比較対照を行った。これに，語彙リストが示されていた時代の学習指導要領に変わることなく採用され続けた動詞80語をかけ合わせると，日本人英語初学者にとって「欠かせない動詞群」が姿を現した。

　これらの動詞を用いることで，英語の基本構造の学習は過不足なくできるはずであることを提案した。このような背景を持つ語彙リストを提案することはこれまでには無かったことである。

　教科用図書の作成者は，教材を作成する際に，この語彙リストを参照し，clause typeごとに示した動詞の種類を勘案しながら言語材料としての語彙のチェックができるはずである。日本人英語初学者にとって難しいと思われる語彙がある場合，この語彙リストにある語で置き換えることも可能である。

　本書ではLDOCEの1番目に挙げられた語義のみを取り上げて，clause typeを確かめる方式を取ったが，これを2番目，3番目の語義にまで広げる場合，clause typeの分布の割合がどのように変化するかを確認する必要がある。さらに，類義性を持った語のグループにおいて，その中のいずれ

を「基本動詞」として採用するかについての議論は行っていない。これらは今後の課題である。

　本書では，「語彙学習の在り方・進め方」も検討の課題から外した。これは，本書で示した「語彙リスト」と関連させて，類義語間のコア性の確認と，同一語における多義間のコア性の在り方の確認，またこれら両者の関連を明らかにすることで，「基本動詞」の選び方に新たな視点を加えることができると考えている。勿論，語彙学習の在り方への追求も今後の課題である。

参 考 文 献

相澤一美・石川慎一郎・村田年. (編集代表). (2005). 『「大学英語教育学会基本語リスト」に基づくJACET8000英単語』東京：桐原書店.

安藤貞雄. (2005). 『現代英文法講義：Lectures on Modern English Grammar』東京：開拓社.

安藤貞雄. (2008). 『英語の文型：文型がわかれば，英語がわかる』東京：開拓社.

安藤昭一他. (編). (1991). 『英語教育現代キーワード事典』大阪：増進堂.

Biber, D., Johansson, S., Leech, G., Conrad, S., & Finegan, E. (1999). *Longman grammar of spoken and written English.* Harlow, Essex: Pearson Education.

The British Component of the International Corpus of English (Release 2) [Computer software]. (2006). London: The Survey of English Usage, University College London.

Carter, R. (1998). *Vocabulary: Applied linguistic perspectives* (2nd ed.). London: Routledge.

Carter, R. (2001). Vocabulary. In R. Carter & D. Nunan (Eds.), *The Cambridge guide to teaching English to speakers of other languages* (pp.42-48). Cambridge: Cambridge University Press.

Carter, R., & McCarthy, M. (1988). *Vocabulary and language teaching.* London: Longman.

Carter, R., & Nunan, D. (Eds.). (2001). *The Cambridge guide to teaching English to speakers of other languages.* Cambridge: Cambridge University Press.

中央教育研究所. (2002). 『研究報告No.60 平成14年度版中学校英語教科書における語彙調査』東京：中央教育研究所.

Close, R. A. (1977). *English as a foreign language: Its constant grammatical problems* (2nd ed.). London: George Allen & Unwin.

Cook, V. (2001). *Second language learning and language teaching* (3rd ed.). London: Arnold.

大学英語教育学会基本語改訂委員会. (編). (2003). 『大学英語教育学会基本語リスト：JACET List of 8000 Basic Words』東京：大学英語教育学会.

Davies, M., & Gardner, D. (2010). *A frequency dictionary of contemporary American English: Word sketches, collocates, and thematic lists.* London: Routledge.

土岸真由美. (2005). 「中学校における必修語―動詞(1)―」『英語英米文学論集』*14,* 77-92. 安田女子大学英語英米文学会.

土岸真由美. (2005). 「中学校における必修語―動詞(2)―」『安田女子大学大学院文学研究科紀要』*10,* 55-75. 安田女子大学大学院文学研究科.

土岸真由美. (2005). 「中学校における必修語―動詞(3)―：意味のコア性の観点から」『中国地区英語教育学会研究紀要』*35,*29-36.

Dogishi, M. (2006). In search of basic verbs for Japanese learners of EFL at the junior high school level: A view from "coreness." *ARELE: Annual Review of English Language Education in Japan, 17,* 161-170.

土岸真由美. (2007). 「映画『ミセス・ダウト』のスクリプトを用いたclause patternの調査」『英語英米文学論集』*16,* 69-81. 安田女子大学英語英米文学会.

土岸真由美. (2007). 「日本人英語初学者のための基本語彙選定(動詞)―基本的英語文型について―」『安田女子大学大学院文学研究科紀要』*12,* 35-50. 安田女子大学大学院文学研究科.

土岸真由美. (2009). 「中学校学習指導要領に記載された『語彙』の変遷」『安田女子大学大学院文学研究科紀要』*14,* 1-12. 安田女子大学大学院文学研究科.

土岸真由美. (2009). 「日本人英語初学者のための基本動詞選定に関する研究」(博士学位論文)安田女子大学大学院文学研究科.

Ellis, N. C. (1997). Vocabulary acquisition: Word structure, collocation, word-class, and meaning. In N. Schmitt & M. McCarthy (Eds.), *Vocabulary: Description, acquisition and pedagogy* (pp.122-139). Cambridge: Cambridge University Press.

Faucett, L., & Maki, I. (1932). *A study of English word-values statistically determined from the latest extensive word-counts: Proving teachers and students with a means of distinguishing indispensable, essential, and useful words from special words.* Tokyo: Matsumura Sanshodo.

Fries, C. C. (1945). *Teaching and learning English as a foreign language.* Ann Arbor, MI: The University of Michigan Press.

Fries, C. C., & Fries, A. C. (1961). *Foundations for English teaching: Including a corpus of materials upon which to build textbooks and teachers' guides for teaching English in Japan.* Tokyo: Kenkyusha.

Fries, C. C., & Traver, A. A. (1950). *English word lists: A study of their adaptability for instruction.* Ann Arbor, MI: The George Wahr.

長谷川潔・小池生夫・島岡丘・竹蓋幸生．(編)．(1988)．『プロシード英和辞典』東京：福武書店．

平田和人．(編著)．(2008)．『中学校新学習指導要領の展開：外国語科英語編』東京：明治図書．

The International Phonetic Association. (1999). *Handbook of the international phonetic association: A guide to the use of the international phonetic alphabet.* Cambridge: Cambridge University Press.

Jackson, H. (2002). *Grammar and vocabulary: A resource book for students.* London: Routledge.

門田修平．(編著)．池村大一郎・中西義子・野呂忠司・島本たい子・横川博一．(2003)．『英語のメンタルレキシコン：語彙の獲得・処理・学習』東京：松柏社．

景山太郎．(編)．(2001)．『日英対照 動詞の意味と構文』東京：大修館．

金田道和．(2007)．「フリーズ理論再訪(6)：『ファウンデーションズの意味するもの』(2)」『安田女子大学大学院文学研究科紀要』*12*, 23-34. 安田女子大学大学院文学研究科．

教育情報ナショナルセンター．http://www.nicer.go.jp/

Leech, G., Rayson, P., & Wilson, A. (2001). *Word frequencies in written and spoken English: Based on the British national corpus.* Harlow, England: Pearson Education.

McArthur, T. (1981). *Longman lexicon of contemporary English.* Harlow, Essex: Longman.

文部科学省．http://www.mext.go.jp/a_menu/shotou/new-cs/index.htm

文部科学省. (2008). 『中学校学習指導要領』京都：東山書房.

文部科学省. (2008). 『中学校学習指導要領解説：外国語編』東京：開隆堂.

文部省. (1959). 『中学校外国語［英語］指導書』東京：開隆堂.

文部省. (1970). 『中学校指導書：外国語編』東京：開隆堂.

文部省. (1978). 『中学校指導書：外国語編』東京：開隆堂.

文部省. (1989). 『中学校指導書：外国語編』東京：開隆堂.

文部省. (1999). 『中学校学習指導要領解説：外国語編』東京：東京書籍.

Nation, I. S. P. (1990). *Teaching and learning vocabulary.* Boston, MA: Heinle & Heinle.

Nation, I. S. P. (2001). *Learning vocabulary in another language.* Cambridge: Cambridge University Press.

Nation, P., & Waring, R. (1997). Vocabulary size, text coverage and word lists. In N. Schmitt & M. McCarthy (Eds.), *Vocabulary: Description, acquisition and pedagogy* (pp.6-19). Cambridge: Cambridge University Press.

Nelson, G., Wallis, S., & Aarts, B. (2002). *Exploring natural language: Working with the British component of the international corpus of English.* Amsterdam: John Benjamins.

日本教材システム編集部. (編). (2008). 『ひと目でわかる 2 色刷り 中学校学習指導要領 新旧比較対照表：平成10年版×平成20年版』東京：教育出版.

Nunan, D. (2001). Second language acquisition. In R. Carter & D. Nunan (Eds.), *The Cambridge guide to teaching English to speakers of other languages* (pp.87-92). Cambridge: Cambridge University Press.

大村喜吉・高梨健吉・出来成訓. (編). (1980). 『英語教育史資料 第 1 巻：英語教育課程の変遷』東京：東京法令出版.

小野経男. (2007). 『英語類義動詞の構文事典』東京：大修館.

Quirk, R., Greenbaum, S., Leech, G., & Svartvik, J. (1985). *A comprehensive grammar of the English language.* Harlow, Essex: Pearson Education.

Richards, I. A. (1943). *Basic English and its uses.* London: Kegan Paul.

Schmitt, N. (2000). *Vocabulary in language teaching.* Cambridge: Cambridge University Press.

Schmitt, N., & McCarthy, M. (Eds.). (1997). *Vocabulary: Description, acquisition and pedagogy.* Cambridge: Cambridge University Press.

Summers, D., et al. (Eds.). (2003). *Longman dictionary of contemporary English* (4th ed.). Harlow, Essex: Pearson Education.

竹蓋幸生. (編). (1994).『言語行動の研究』*4*. 千葉大学英語学・言語行動研究会.

竹蓋幸生・中條清美. (1994).「語彙リスト:『現代英語のキーワード』―その開発と有効度の検証―」竹蓋幸生(編),『言語行動の研究』*4* (pp.2-24). 千葉大学英語学・言語行動研究会.

田中茂範・武田修一・川出才紀. (編). (2003).『Eゲイト英和辞典』東京: Benesse.

寺澤芳雄. (1981).『Longman LEXICON of Contemporary English 解説:特色と使い方』丸善株式会社. (McArthur, T.［1981］に付属)

投野由紀夫. (編著). (1997).『英語語彙習得論:ボキャブラリー学習を科学する』東京:河源社.

馬本勉. (2001).「日本の英語教育における基本語の選定基準に関する研究―定義可能度を中心として―」(博士学位論文)広島大学大学院教育研究科.

Webster's new dictionary of synonyms: A dictionary of discriminated synonyms with antonyms and analogous and contrasted words. (1984). Springfield, MA: Merriam-Webster.

West, M. (1953). *A general service list of English words: With semantic frequencies and a supplementary word-list for the writing of popular science and technology.* Harlow, Essex: Longman.

付　録

付録1．ICE-GBの動詞

ICE-GBのclause typeごとの動詞の一覧を以下に挙げる。各語の左側の数字が通し番号を表し，右側の数値がICE-GBにおけるその語の出現頻度を表している。

Intransitive

1	be	4,135	22	stand	185	43	play	112
2	go	2,567	23	turn	181	44	lie1	110
3	come	1,838	24	lead	179	45	result	109
4	say	1,400	25	wait	170	46	refer	107
5	think	932	26	try	164	47	suppose	100
6	look	890	27	stay	155	48	rise	99
7	work	639	28	walk	153	49	ask	96
8	get	629	29	depend	150	50	pay	91
9	know	620	30	fall	148	51	seem	90
10	happen	521	31	deal	145	52	act	85
11	talk	472	32	die	144	53	break	85
12	do	368	33	apply	135	54	suffer	85
13	live	367	34	change	134	55	continue	84
14	move	307	35	exist	134	56	leave	84
15	speak	281	36	hear	134	57	increase	81
16	run	251	37	appear	129	58	return	81
17	write	248	38	grow	128	59	follow	78
18	start	244	39	arrive	124	60	matter	78
19	sit	239	40	agree	121	61	remember	75
20	occur	231	41	listen	119	62	meet	73
21	see	208	42	begin	117	63	operate	72

64	travel	72		97	close	45		130	belong	31
65	believe	71		98	rely	45		131	draw	31
66	arise	69		99	fail	44		132	focus	31
67	emerge	69		100	hold	44		133	allow	30
68	call	67		101	fly	42		134	evolve	30
69	pass	67		102	point	42		135	head	30
70	stop	67		103	set	42		136	cut	29
71	remain	66		104	contribute	41		137	escape	29
72	end	64		105	fit	41		138	mind	29
73	take	63		106	flow	41		139	open	29
74	develop	62		107	mean	41		140	proceed	29
75	respond	61		108	ring	41		141	progress	29
76	disappear	60		109	compete	40		142	account	28
77	hang	59		110	hope	40		143	jump	28
78	help	59		111	behave	39		144	step	28
79	read	59		112	care	38		145	build	27
80	report	59		113	learn	38		146	check	27
81	add	58		114	sing	38		147	complain	27
82	last	58		115	eat	37		148	date	27
83	like	57		116	show	37		149	give	27
84	relate	56		117	drop	36		150	lose	27
85	worry	56		118	explain	36		151	rest	27
86	drive	55		119	sleep	36		152	serve	27
87	vary	55		120	understand	35		153	stick	27
88	cope	54		121	argue	34		154	wander	27
89	succeed	53		122	dance	34		155	communicate	26
90	concentrate	50		123	decide	34		156	expand	26
91	fight	48		124	settle	34		157	differ	25
92	survive	48		125	have	33		158	feel	25
93	vote	48		126	pull	33		159	forget	25
94	win	47		127	benefit	32		160	guess	25
95	consist	46		128	find	32		161	imagine	25
96	finish	46		129	wonder	32		162	make	25

163	perform	25	196	recover	20	229	record	16
164	phone	25	197	sink	20	230	reply	16
165	push	25	198	tell	20	231	shut	16
166	react	25	199	watch	20	232	admit	15
167	smile	25	200	blow	19	233	amount	15
168	study	25	201	breathe	19	234	catch	15
169	teach	25	202	drift	19	235	decrease	15
170	comment	24	203	nod	19	236	dress	15
171	extend	24	204	originate	19	237	gather	15
172	improve	24	205	paint	19	238	prevail	15
173	lean	24	206	process	19	239	resign	15
174	qualify	24	207	retire	19	240	specialize	15
175	shout	24	208	suggest	19	241	clear	14
176	collapse	23	209	apologize	18	242	compare	14
177	laugh	23	210	carry	18	243	cook	14
178	burst	22	211	feed	18	244	engage	14
179	insist	22	212	form	18	245	invest	14
180	join	22	213	miss	18	246	object	14
181	rush	22	214	range	18	247	participate	14
182	slip	22	215	struggle	18	248	quote	14
183	appeal	21	216	cease	17	249	realize	14
184	attend	21	217	claim	17	250	slide	14
185	count	21	218	cry	17	251	spend	14
186	decline	21	219	marry	17	252	tend	14
187	roll	21	220	ride	17	253	choose	13
188	sell	21	221	stare	17	254	climb	13
189	spread	21	222	buy	16	255	cost	13
190	switch	21	223	enter	16	256	dry	13
191	use	21	224	intervene	16	257	judge	13
192	withdraw	21	225	keep	16	258	march	13
193	land	20	226	pop	16	259	negotiate	13
194	pick	20	227	prepare	16	260	notice	13
195	reach	20	228	press	16	261	provide	13

262	reflect	13		295	derive	11		328	graduate	9
263	search	13		296	distinguish	11		329	hesitate	9
264	shoot	13		297	expire	11		330	link	9
265	swim	13		298	face	11		331	persist	9
266	swing	13		299	glance	11		332	plead	9
267	wake	13		300	hurt	11		333	rule	9
268	wash	13		301	kick	11		334	sail	9
269	wear	13		302	peer	11		335	share	9
270	advise	12		303	retaliate	11		336	sign	9
271	bounce	12		304	shine	11		337	spin	9
272	chat	12		305	spring	11		338	state	9
273	comply	12		306	want	11		339	stretch	9
274	correspond	12		307	approach	10		340	stumble	9
275	disagree	12		308	burn	10		341	suspect	9
276	embark	12		309	cross	10		342	sweep	9
277	fill	12		310	dribble	10		343	aim	8
278	interact	12		311	expect	10		344	answer	8
279	interfere	12		312	float	10		345	beg	8
280	knock	12		313	function	10		346	bend	8
281	manage	12		314	indicate	10		347	bowl	8
282	opt	12		315	note	10		348	bump	8
283	put	12		316	recall	10		349	circulate	8
284	rain	12		317	repeat	10		350	coincide	8
285	weigh	12		318	save	10		351	divide	8
286	accelerate	11		319	scream	10		352	double	8
287	adapt	11		320	split	10		353	dwell	8
288	advance	11		321	swell	10		354	explode	8
289	bear	11		322	throw	10		355	fire	8
290	book	11		323	touch	10		356	flee	8
291	bother	11		324	centre	9		357	lecture	8
292	cling	11		325	creep	9		358	lie2	8
293	cool	11		326	dispose	9		359	migrate	8
294	degenerate	11		327	dream	9		360	pour	8

361	reside	8	394	mention	7	427	converse	6
362	score	8	395	mix	7	428	cover	6
363	slow	8	396	moan	7	429	crack	6
364	stride	8	397	part	7	430	crawl	6
365	submit	8	398	pause	7	431	cycle	6
366	surrender	8	399	plan	7	432	declare	6
367	trade	8	400	race	7	433	depart	6
368	train	8	401	rally	7	434	differentiate	6
369	tumble	8	402	reappear	7	435	dip	6
370	wish	8	403	rot	7	436	discover	6
371	accumulate	7	404	shot	7	437	discriminate	6
372	adhere	7	405	smoke	7	438	drain	6
373	arrange	7	406	sound	7	439	ease	6
374	assist	7	407	spill	7	440	evaporate	6
375	attack	7	408	sue	7	441	experiment	6
376	back	7	409	test	7	442	fade	6
377	borrow	7	410	thrive	7	443	fish	6
378	combine	7	411	trust	7	444	fold	6
379	commence	7	412	tune	7	445	freeze	6
380	compensate	7	413	volunteer	7	446	glide	6
381	cooperate	7	414	balance	6	447	govern	6
382	culminate	7	415	blame	6	448	hint	6
383	diminish	7	416	breed	6	449	hit	6
384	drown	7	417	broadcast	6	450	identify	6
385	flourish	7	418	bud	6	451	indulge	6
386	heat	7	419	charge	6	452	malinger	6
387	hover	7	420	chase	6	453	mature	6
388	inquire	7	421	clean	6	454	merge	6
389	investigate	7	422	collaborate	6	455	milk	6
390	joke	7	423	concede	6	456	overlap	6
391	leap	7	424	confess	6	457	pack	6
392	loom	7	425	confide	6	458	panic	6
393	manoeuvre	7	426	converge	6	459	pray	6

460	redominate	6	493	descend	5	526	shuffle	5
461	program	6	494	determine	5	527	sigh	5
462	protest	6	495	detract	5	528	skip	5
463	relax	6	496	enroll	5	529	smell	5
464	retreat	6	497	fear	5	530	sob	5
465	roar	6	498	foster	5	531	speed	5
466	snap	6	499	gain	5	532	starve	5
467	soar	6	500	gaze	5	533	stem	5
468	speculate	6	501	grind	5	534	stream	5
469	stray	6	502	hide	5	535	summarize	5
470	strike	6	503	hurry	5	536	surface	5
471	tidy	6	504	leak	5	537	tie	5
472	trail	6	505	let go	5	538	vanish	5
473	tread	6	506	lift	5	539	vibrate	5
474	trot	6	507	light	5	540	visit	5
475	type	6	508	linger	5	541	wave	5
476	unfold	6	509	measure	5	542	word process	5
477	venture	6	510	mess	5	543	wriggle	5
478	warm	6	511	penetrate	5	544	yawn	5
479	weaken	6	512	receive	5	545	adjust	4
480	weep	6	513	reckon	5	546	advertise	4
481	abound	5	514	refrain	5	547	allude	4
482	bite	5	515	regenerate	5	548	aspire	4
483	blossom	5	516	remark	5	549	backtrack	4
484	campaign	5	517	revolve	5	550	ball	4
485	chip	5	518	root	5	551	bat	4
486	collect	5	519	sag	5	552	bleed	4
487	conclude	5	520	salute	5	553	boil	4
488	confirm	5	521	send	5	554	bow	4
489	conform	5	522	separate	5	555	brake	4
490	contract	5	523	shave	5	556	calm	4
491	control	5	524	shift	5	557	cancel	4
492	default	5	525	shop	5	558	chill	4

559	coalesce	4	592	hack	4	625	signal	4
560	collide	4	593	halt	4	626	ski	4
561	compromise	4	594	handle	4	627	slump	4
562	conceive	4	595	hot	4	628	stabilize	4
563	condense	4	596	dustrialize	4	629	stamp	4
564	conflict	4	597	innovate	4	630	stir	4
565	conspired	4	598	invade	4	631	straighten	4
566	contrast	4	599	kill	4	632	swallow	4
567	correlate	4	600	labour	4	633	sweat	4
568	crash	4	601	lapse	4	634	swot	4
569	crumble	4	602	lie3	4	635	sympathise	4
570	deepen	4	603	lunch	4	636	terminate	4
571	demonstrate	4	604	materialise	4	637	tour	4
572	describe	4	605	melt	4	638	transpire	4
573	detect	4	606	narrow	4	639	twist	4
574	disintegrate	4	607	observe	4	640	unite	4
575	disperse	4	608	ooze	4	641	whip	4
576	dive	4	609	plummet	4	642	whisper	4
577	drill	4	610	pontificate	4	643	whiz	4
578	drink	4	611	pounce	4	644	widen	4
579	edge	4	612	preside	4	645	yearn	4
580	elapse	4	613	protrude	4	646	<unclear-word>	3
581	emigrate	4	614	recede	4	647	abide	3
582	encroach	4	615	recur	4	648	accept	3
583	entertain	4	616	refuse	4	649	accord	3
584	exit	4	617	register	4	650	acknowledge	3
585	export	4	618	rehearse	4	651	approve	3
586	extrude	4	619	resort	4	652	approximate	3
587	feature	4	620	revert	4	653	assemble	3
588	fiddle	4	621	rotate	4	654	assume	3
589	flare	4	622	shape	4	655	atrophy	3
590	flick	4	623	shrink	4	656	average	3
591	frown	4	624	side	4	657	backfire	3

658	bank	3
659	battle	3
660	blink	3
661	burrow	3
662	capitalise	3
663	carve	3
664	cater	3
665	celebrate	3
666	challenge	3
667	cheat	3
668	clap	3
669	clot	3
670	club	3
671	coach	3
672	consult	3
673	create	3
674	crouch	3
675	cruise	3
676	dawn	3
677	decay	3
678	defecate	3
679	defend	3
680	deflect	3
681	delay	3
682	demand	3
683	design	3
684	deteriorate	3
685	digress	3
686	disapprove	3
687	dissolve	3
688	dither	3
689	echo	3
690	elaborate	3

691	emanate	3
692	emphasize	3
693	falter	3
694	fasten	3
695	figure	3
696	film	3
697	filter	3
698	flinch	3
699	flip	3
700	flood	3
701	flower	3
702	flutter	3
703	froth	3
704	fry	3
705	fuck	3
706	fuss	3
707	graze	3
708	grieve	3
709	grill	3
710	grin	3
711	groan	3
712	group	3
713	grumble	3
714	gush	3
715	harden	3
716	heal	3
717	hum	3
718	illustrate	3
719	import	3
720	inflate	3
721	kid	3
722	lack	3
723	lag	3

724	liaise	3
725	long	3
726	lurch	3
727	lurk	3
728	map	3
729	mimic	3
730	mingle	3
731	mutter	3
732	nag	3
733	nest	3
734	nick	3
735	nip	3
736	obtain	3
737	officiate	3
738	owe	3
739	park	3
740	peel	3
741	peep	3
742	permit	3
743	place	3
744	plunge	3
745	ponder	3
746	preach	3
747	present	3
748	pretend	3
749	print	3
750	profit	3
751	propose	3
752	prosecute	3
753	prosper	3
754	purchase	3
755	queue	3
756	recruit	3

757	relapse	3	790	accrue	2	823	commute	2
758	restart	3	791	adopt	2	824	compere	2
759	revise	3	792	aid	2	825	complete	2
760	rub	3	793	alternate	2	826	conduct	2
761	seep	3	794	anticipate	2	827	connect	2
762	shake	3	795	assess	2	828	contend	2
763	shatter	3	796	associate	2	829	convert	2
764	shiver	3	797	attach	2	830	correct	2
765	shudder	3	798	await	2	831	crave	2
766	simmer	3	799	bang	2	832	cringe	2
767	sort	3	800	bark	2	833	crow	2
768	spell	3	801	beat	2	834	curl	2
769	squat	3	802	beckon	2	835	curve	2
770	stagger	3	803	bet	2	836	dash	2
771	stall	3	804	bid	2	837	daydream	2
772	storm	3	805	bind	2	838	decussate	2
773	swarm	3	806	bleat	2	839	define	2
774	swear	3	807	blunder	2	840	delight	2
775	tape	3	808	boom	2	841	desert	2
776	telephone	3	809	bore	2	842	desire	2
777	thin	3	810	bottle	2	843	despair	2
778	tire	3	811	brag	2	844	dig	2
779	track	3	812	brood	2	845	discuss	2
780	tremble	3	813	bubble	2	846	disguise	2
781	tug	3	814	buckle	2	847	dissociate	2
782	vomit	3	815	calculate	2	848	divert	2
783	wallow	3	816	carp	2	849	divorce	2
784	wane	3	817	chant	2	850	doodle	2
785	waver	3	818	cheer	2	851	drag	2
786	wind	3	819	chuck	2	852	drip	2
787	absorb	2	820	clatter	2	853	ebb	2
788	abstain	2	821	coexist	2	854	economise	2
789	accommodate	2	822	cohabit	2	855	enlarge	2

856	enthuse	2	889	gossip	2	922	loop	2
857	equalise	2	890	haggle	2	923	lust	2
858	erupt	2	891	halve	2	924	malfunction	2
859	establish	2	892	hare	2	925	manufacture	2
860	estimate	2	893	harp	2	926	march past	2
861	examine	2	894	hatch	2	927	match	2
862	exchange	2	895	hitchhike	2	928	meander	2
863	exercise	2	896	home	2	929	misbehave	2
864	extract	2	897	hone	2	930	mist	2
865	extrapolate	2	898	hop	2	931	modernize	2
866	fare	2	899	hug	2	932	mount	2
867	farm	2	900	hunt	2	933	mourn	2
868	fend	2	901	hurdle	2	934	multiply	2
869	file	2	902	illuminate	2	935	mumble	2
870	fizz	2	903	impact	2	936	navigate	2
871	flag	2	904	incline	2	937	offer	2
872	flash	2	905	integrate	2	938	oppose	2
873	flock	2	906	intend	2	939	over-expand	2
874	flop	2	907	intensify	2	940	overflow	2
875	fluctuate	2	908	interpret	2	941	over-heat	2
876	founder	2	909	intrude	2	942	own	2
877	fracture	2	910	invent	2	943	pace	2
878	fragment	2	911	isolate	2	944	pander	2
879	fumble	2	912	issue	2	945	perish	2
880	gallop	2	913	jog	2	946	photocopy	2
881	gamble	2	914	jut	2	947	pile	2
882	gape	2	915	key-punch	2	948	poke	2
883	gel	2	916	launch	2	949	police	2
884	generalize	2	917	lengthen	2	950	power	2
885	generate	2	918	let	2	951	practice	2
886	germinate	2	919	load	2	952	predict	2
887	gesticulate	2	920	locate	2	953	prefer	2
888	gloss	2	921	lock	2	954	produce	2

955	proliferate	2	988	scramble	2	1021	strive	2
956	proofread	2	989	scrape	2	1022	stroll	2
957	publish	2	990	screech	2	1023	subscribe	2
958	quibble	2	991	screw	2	1024	subside	2
959	quick march	2	992	scroll	2	1025	subsist	2
960	rage	2	993	season	2	1026	substitute	2
961	ramble	2	994	seek	2	1027	succumb	2
962	rank	2	995	select	2	1028	suffice	2
963	rate	2	996	sheer	2	1029	suffocate	2
964	ratify	2	997	shelter	2	1030	suit	2
965	re-apply	2	998	shriek	2	1031	sway	2
966	rebound	2	999	shy	2	1032	swerve	2
967	rebuild	2	1000	skate	2	1033	swivel	2
968	reduce	2	1001	sketch	2	1034	tangle	2
969	reign	2	1002	skid	2	1035	tender	2
970	remove	2	1003	skulk	2	1036	testify	2
971	re-open	2	1004	slop	2	1037	thaw	2
972	repair	2	1005	slope	2	1038	thrust	2
973	request	2	1006	slow march	2	1039	thud	2
974	resist	2	1007	sneak	2	1040	tighten	2
975	resonate	2	1008	sniff	2	1041	tilt	2
976	resume	2	1009	snodgrass	2	1042	totter	2
977	revel	2	1010	snore	2	1043	tower	2
978	reverse	2	1011	snow	2	1044	transmit	2
979	revive	2	1012	solo	2	1045	treble	2
980	right foot	2	1013	spiral	2	1046	trespass	2
981	roam	2	1014	sprint	2	1047	trickle	2
982	row	2	1015	squeeze	2	1048	trip	2
983	rumble	2	1016	squirm	2	1049	troop	2
984	sand	2	1017	steer	2	1050	trundle	2
985	scab	2	1018	stock	2	1051	tussle	2
986	scan	2	1019	stoop	2	1052	veer	2
987	scatter	2	1020	strip	2	1053	vie	2

1054	view	2		1087	attract	1		1120	bode	1
1055	voice	2		1088	audition	1		1121	bond	1
1056	volley	2		1089	augur	1		1122	border	1
1057	wail	2		1090	awake	1		1123	breast beat	1
1058	warble	2		1091	a-woo	1		1124	breeze	1
1059	water	2		1092	baby-sit	1		1125	brick	1
1060	whirl	2		1093	back space	1		1126	brim	1
1061	wince	2		1094	backpack	1		1127	broil	1
1062	wobble	2		1095	balloon	1		1128	brush	1
1063	wrestle	2		1096	bargain	1		1129	bucket	1
1064	about turn	1		1097	bask	1		1130	budget	1
1065	accede	1		1098	bathe	1		1131	bunch	1
1066	accompany	1		1099	batter	1		1132	burble	1
1067	accuse	1		1100	become	1		1133	burp	1
1068	ache	1		1101	befall	1		1134	bustle	1
1069	achieve	1		1102	beginnen	1		1135	camp	1
1070	administrate	1		1103	behold	1		1136	cannon	1
1071	advert	1		1104	beware	1		1137	canter	1
1072	aggrade	1		1105	bicycle	1		1138	career	1
1073	aggregate	1		1106	bill	1		1139	caress	1
1074	align	1		1107	bipolarise	1		1140	carouse	1
1075	allege	1		1108	bird-watch	1		1141	carve	1
1076	alter	1		1109	bitch	1		1142	cast	1
1077	analyse	1		1110	blank	1		1143	cat-sit	1
1078	anneal	1		1111	blaze	1		1144	caution	1
1079	appreciate	1		1112	bless	1		1145	cavil	1
1080	arbitrate	1		1113	blindfold	1		1146	cavort	1
1081	arch	1		1114	blob	1		1147	chatter	1
1082	arse-lick	1		1115	block	1		1148	chew	1
1083	ascend	1		1116	bloom	1		1149	chime	1
1084	ascertain	1		1117	bluff	1		1150	chop	1
1085	asphyxiate	1		1118	blush	1		1151	choreography	1
1086	attest	1		1119	board	1		1152	churn	1

1153	cite	1		1186	counsel	1		1219	dine	1
1154	clash	1		1187	counter-attack	1		1220	disappoint	1
1155	clasp	1		1188	crackle	1		1221	discharge	1
1156	cleave	1		1189	crease	1		1222	discommon	1
1157	clench	1		1190	credit	1		1223	disentangle	1
1158	clip	1		1191	croak	1		1224	disregard	1
1159	cluster	1		1192	crown	1		1225	disseminate	1
1160	clutch	1		1193	crunch	1		1226	dissent	1
1161	cobble	1		1194	cultivate	1		1227	distract	1
1162	cockle	1		1195	curse	1		1228	diverge	1
1163	code	1		1196	dangle	1		1229	diversify	1
1164	cogitate	1		1197	darn	1		1230	dodge	1
1165	cohere	1		1198	dart	1		1231	dominate	1
1166	commiserate	1		1199	dawdle	1		1232	donate	1
1167	commune	1		1200	dazzle	1		1233	dot	1
1168	compile	1		1201	debug	1		1234	double-check	1
1169	compose	1		1202	decipher	1		1235	doubt	1
1170	compost	1		1203	decompose	1		1236	draft	1
1171	comprehend	1		1204	decorate	1		1237	drum	1
1172	compute	1		1205	delete	1		1238	duck	1
1173	congeal	1		1206	deliberate	1		1239	dwindle	1
1174	conjure	1		1207	delineate	1		1240	earn	1
1175	consent	1		1208	demur	1		1241	eat eat eat	1
1176	consider	1		1209	deny	1		1242	eaves-drop	1
1177	console	1		1210	deploy	1		1243	edit	1
1178	consolidate	1		1211	depose	1		1244	elongate	1
1179	construct	1		1212	deputise	1		1245	embroider	1
1180	contact	1		1213	detach	1		1246	empire build	1
1181	contrive	1		1214	diagnose	1		1247	employ	1
1182	convince	1		1215	dial	1		1248	empty	1
1183	coo	1		1216	dichotomise	1		1249	enact	1
1184	core	1		1217	diffuse	1		1250	endure	1
1185	corner	1		1218	digest	1		1251	enforce	1

1252	engorge	1
1253	enrich	1
1254	ensue	1
1255	erase	1
1256	erode	1
1257	even	1
1258	exaggerate	1
1259	excel	1
1260	exclaim	1
1261	exhibit	1
1262	exploit	1
1263	explore	1
1264	facilitate	1
1265	fantasize	1
1266	fecit	1
1267	fine	1
1268	fix	1
1269	fixate	1
1270	flail	1
1271	flake	1
1272	flatten	1
1273	flicker	1
1274	flirt	1
1275	flounce	1
1276	flounder	1
1277	flush	1
1278	foretell	1
1279	forfeit	1
1280	forge	1
1281	forgive	1
1282	fork	1
1283	freewheel	1
1284	fret	1

1285	frighten	1
1286	frolic	1
1287	fudge	1
1288	fuse	1
1289	gallivant	1
1290	garden	1
1291	gasp	1
1292	gass	1
1293	gatecrash	1
1294	gawp	1
1295	gesture	1
1296	giggle	1
1297	glare	1
1298	glint	1
1299	glow	1
1300	glowe	1
1301	glue	1
1302	graft	1
1303	grant	1
1304	grapple	1
1305	gravitate	1
1306	groove	1
1307	grovel	1
1308	growl	1
1309	grunt	1
1310	guard	1
1311	guesstimate	1
1312	guest	1
1313	gully	1
1314	hail	1
1315	half-fall	1
1316	hammer	1
1317	hand	1

1318	handicap	1
1319	hark	1
1320	harm	1
1321	harrow	1
1322	hasten	1
1323	haw	1
1324	hibernate	1
1325	hike	1
1326	hill-walk	1
1327	hiss	1
1328	hitch	1
1329	hobble	1
1330	hook	1
1331	howl	1
1332	huddle	1
1333	hurtle	1
1334	hyperpolarise	1
1335	hypnotise	1
1336	impinge	1
1337	implement	1
1338	include	1
1339	index	1
1340	inform	1
1341	inhabit	1
1342	initiate	1
1343	injure	1
1344	inspect	1
1345	instruct	1
1346	insure	1
1347	intercept	1
1348	interview	1
1349	introduce	1
1350	inveigh	1

1351	invoice	1	1384	love	1	1417	orbit	1
1352	iron	1	1385	make do	1	1418	organize	1
1353	irrigate	1	1386	manifest	1	1419	oscillate	1
1354	irrupt	1	1387	market	1	1420	outflank	1
1355	jabber	1	1388	marshal	1	1421	outline	1
1356	jeer	1	1389	mediate	1	1422	oven bake	1
1357	jerk	1	1390	mellow	1	1423	overlay	1
1358	jet-set	1	1391	menstruate	1	1424	overpass	1
1359	jib	1	1392	metamorphose	1	1425	override	1
1360	jibe	1	1393	militate	1	1426	overspill	1
1361	jink	1	1394	model	1	1427	overtake	1
1362	joggle	1	1395	moderate	1	1428	overturn	1
1363	jostle	1	1396	monitor	1	1429	p.t.o	1
1364	jounce	1	1397	moon	1	1430	paddle	1
1365	journey	1	1398	moot	1	1431	page	1
1366	kiss	1	1399	muck	1	1432	pale	1
1367	kneel	1	1400	muddle	1	1433	palm	1
1368	knife	1	1401	multi-task	1	1434	paper	1
1369	knit	1	1402	muscle	1	1435	parachute	1
1370	kow-tow	1	1403	muse	1	1436	parade	1
1371	lash	1	1404	mushroom	1	1437	partake	1
1372	latch	1	1405	mute	1	1438	pat	1
1373	lease	1	1406	n.b.	1	1439	patent	1
1374	legislate	1	1407	need	1	1440	patrol	1
1375	lend	1	1408	net	1	1441	peak	1
1376	level	1	1409	network	1	1442	pedal	1
1377	lick	1	1410	niggle	1	1443	peg	1
1378	line	1	1411	nose-pick	1	1444	persevere	1
1379	list	1	1412	nurture	1	1445	persuade	1
1380	listen listen listen	1	1413	oblige	1	1446	pertain	1
1381	lobby	1	1414	occured occurred	1	1447	petition	1
1382	lodge	1	1415	offend	1	1448	pine	1
1383	lounge	1	1416	ogle	1	1449	piss	1

1450	please	1
1451	plod	1
1452	plough	1
1453	pluck	1
1454	plug	1
1455	poise	1
1456	pose	1
1457	posture	1
1458	pound	1
1459	precede	1
1460	preclude	1
1461	prescribe	1
1462	prey	1
1463	prick	1
1464	prickle	1
1465	privatise	1
1466	probe	1
1467	project	1
1468	promise	1
1469	pronounce	1
1470	propagandise	1
1471	propagate	1
1472	propound	1
1473	protect	1
1474	pry	1
1475	pulsate	1
1476	pummel	1
1477	punish	1
1478	put paid	1
1479	puzzle	1
1480	quail	1
1481	quarrel	1
1482	quaver	1
1483	question	1
1484	quieten	1
1485	quit	1
1486	radio	1
1487	raise	1
1488	ram	1
1489	rankle	1
1490	rape	1
1491	rationalise	1
1492	rattle	1
1493	ravage	1
1494	readjust	1
1495	re-advertise	1
1496	rear	1
1497	reason	1
1498	reassemble	1
1499	rebel	1
1500	recap	1
1501	recognize	1
1502	recommence	1
1503	recommend	1
1504	reconcile	1
1505	reconnect	1
1506	recount	1
1507	re-emerge	1
1508	refocus	1
1509	re-form	1
1510	regress	1
1511	reinvest	1
1512	rejoin	1
1513	rekit	1
1514	relent	1
1515	relicense	1
1516	relocate	1
1517	remind	1
1518	renege	1
1519	renew	1
1520	rent	1
1521	reorganize	1
1522	repay	1
1523	rephrase	1
1524	repossess	1
1525	reprocess	1
1526	require	1
1527	research	1
1528	reshoot	1
1529	resound	1
1530	respire	1
1531	re-take	1
1532	retest	1
1533	retort	1
1534	reunite	1
1535	reverberate	1
1536	rewrite	1
1537	ricochet	1
1538	rift	1
1539	righten	1
1540	rip	1
1541	ripen	1
1542	rock	1
1543	roller skate	1
1544	room	1
1545	roost	1
1546	row/column scan	1
1547	rupture	1
1548	rust	1

1549	safeguard	1	1582	smash	1	1615	stump	1
1550	salivate	1	1583	smooch	1	1616	stutter	1
1551	satirise	1	1584	snarl	1	1617	subdue	1
1552	scorch	1	1585	snitch	1	1618	submerge	1
1553	scrabble	1	1586	snog	1	1619	suckle	1
1554	scribble	1	1587	snooze	1	1620	suffuse	1
1555	scuffle	1	1588	snort	1	1621	sulk	1
1556	seduce	1	1589	soften	1	1622	sum	1
1557	senesce	1	1590	sour	1	1623	sunbathe	1
1558	sentence	1	1591	spark	1	1624	support	1
1559	sew	1	1592	spew	1	1625	surge	1
1560	shade	1	1593	splash	1	1626	swagger	1
1561	shallow fry	1	1594	spout	1	1627	swap	1
1562	shape-up	1	1595	sprawl	1	1628	swill	1
1563	sharpen	1	1596	springboard	1	1629	swirl	1
1564	shear	1	1597	spy	1	1630	swish	1
1565	shell	1	1598	square	1	1631	swoop	1
1566	ship-out	1	1599	squeak	1	1632	tag	1
1567	shit	1	1600	squeal	1	1633	tail	1
1568	shorten	1	1601	squint	1	1634	tally	1
1569	shrivel	1	1602	stagnate	1	1635	tamper	1
1570	shrug	1	1603	stalk	1	1636	tap	1
1571	sidle	1	1604	star	1	1637	taper	1
1572	signify	1	1605	steady	1	1638	tax	1
1573	silt	1	1606	steam	1	1639	taxii	1
1574	sitting saying	1	1607	stiffen	1	1640	team	1
1575	skim	1	1608	stimulate	1	1641	teem	1
1576	skimp	1	1609	sting	1	1642	teeter	1
1577	slacken	1	1610	stink	1	1643	theorize	1
1578	slaughter	1	1611	stomp	1	1644	thrash	1
1579	slave	1	1612	straggle	1	1645	throb	1
1580	slink	1	1613	strain	1	1646	throttle	1
1581	slouch	1	1614	strum	1	1647	thump	1

1648	thunder	1
1649	ticket	1
1650	tingle	1
1651	tinker	1
1652	tip	1
1653	toddle	1
1654	toil	1
1655	tone	1
1656	top	1
1657	toss	1
1658	tow	1
1659	toy	1
1660	trace	1
1661	trample	1
1662	transfer	1
1663	transform	1
1664	transit	1
1665	translate	1
1666	treat	1
1667	trek	1
1668	trim	1

1669	triple check	1
1670	triumph	1
1671	trouble	1
1672	trudge	1
1673	tuck	1
1674	twiddle	1
1675	twitch	1
1676	undercut	1
1677	underestimate	1
1678	underline	1
1679	undermine	1
1680	undress	1
1681	unpack	1
1682	unravel	1
1683	unveil	1
1684	uplift	1
1685	upset	1
1686	upturn	1
1687	urge	1
1688	verge	1
1689	wade	1

1690	waffle	1
1691	waggle	1
1692	warn	1
1693	waste	1
1694	wheel	1
1695	whimper	1
1696	whinny	1
1697	whistle	1
1698	whoop	1
1699	wilt	1
1700	wipe	1
1701	wither	1
1702	worsen	1
1703	worship	1
1704	wrangle	1
1705	wrap	1
1706	yell	1
1707	yield	1
1708	zero	1
1709	zip	1
1710	zoom	1

Copular

1	be	29,179
2	become	570
3	look	317
4	get	287
5	feel	273
6	seem	193
7	sound	167
8	remain	144
9	go	73
10	end up	43

11	form	43
12	fall	40
13	prove	39
14	act as	37
15	appear	36
16	comprise	35
17	stay	31
18	constitute	28
19	make up	18
20	come	17

21	grow	17
22	keep	16
23	make	14
24	serve as	12
25	turn out	12
26	lie1	10
27	turn	10
28	taste	9
29	smell	8
30	stand	7

31	consist of	5
32	act	4
33	count as	4
34	come out	3
35	emerge	3
36	run	3
37	take	3
38	weigh	3
39	amount to	2
40	end	2
41	pass	2

42	wax	2
43	amount	1
44	come in	1
45	continue	1
46	cost	1
47	determine	1
48	drop down	1
49	feature	1
50	gleam	1
51	number	1
52	plead	1

53	pose as	1
54	ring	1
55	serve	1
56	spend	1
57	start	1
58	survive	1
59	talk	1
60	turn into	1
61	want	1

Monotransitive

1	have	3,967
2	do	2,568
3	think	2,322
4	say	1,965
5	get	1,927
6	see	1,462
7	take	1,434
8	know	1,377
9	make	1,225
10	use	1,162
11	want	1,104
12	find	633
13	mean	613
14	try	589
15	give	562
16	like	486
17	show	468
18	need	406
19	put	368
20	bring	365

21	provide	365
22	leave	354
23	write	327
24	produce	324
25	pay	310
26	believe	303
27	play	292
28	hear	281
29	remember	278
30	hope	271
31	feel	266
32	read	265
33	involve	237
34	suggest	237
35	meet	234
36	hold	231
37	send	230
38	include	228
39	decide	227
40	carry	222

41	set	221
42	understand	209
43	receive	208
44	require	206
45	buy	200
46	lose	199
47	cause	194
48	consider	191
49	help	184
50	mention	183
51	achieve	181
52	follow	178
53	reach	178
54	change	176
55	spend	175
56	develop	168
57	accept	167
58	seek	165
59	describe	164
60	win	164

61	learn	162	94	kill	115	127	design	86
62	create	157	95	choose	114	128	notice	86
63	build	155	96	pass	114	129	catch	83
64	agree	153	97	thank	114	130	replace	83
65	expect	153	98	sell	113	131	destroy	82
66	ask	151	99	remove	112	132	open	82
67	pick	151	100	assume	111	133	argue	80
68	reduce	151	101	forget	111	134	express	80
69	add	148	102	manage	111	135	compare	79
70	affect	140	103	love	109	136	report	79
71	realize	139	104	hit	108	137	improve	78
72	cover	138	105	introduce	108	138	watch	78
73	increase	138	106	measure	108	139	admit	77
74	keep	138	107	avoid	106	140	break	77
75	offer	138	108	form	103	141	protect	77
76	enjoy	137	109	publish	102	142	save	77
77	explain	135	110	ensure	101	143	determine	76
78	support	135	111	join	101	144	complete	75
79	suppose	135	112	recognize	100	145	obtain	75
80	base	133	113	wonder	99	146	propose	75
81	discuss	133	114	call	98	147	move	74
82	wish	133	115	indicate	98	148	work	72
83	face	131	116	miss	97	149	fill	71
84	raise	131	117	confirm	96	150	reflect	71
85	represent	131	118	present	96	151	serve	71
86	cut	129	119	tell	95	152	apply	70
87	concern	126	120	maintain	94	153	collect	70
88	wear	124	121	start	92	154	employ	70
89	claim	122	122	control	90	155	influence	70
90	establish	119	123	identify	90	156	lay	70
91	draw	118	124	record	90	157	stop	70
92	run	118	125	turn	90	158	associate	69
93	contain	117	126	check	89	159	discover	69

160	examine	68	193	release	60	226	strike	52
161	prevent	68	194	sign	60	227	announce	51
162	share	68	195	adopt	59	228	aim	50
163	enclose	67	196	attend	59	229	suffer	50
164	lead	67	197	display	59	230	appreciate	49
165	point	67	198	eat	59	231	close	49
166	reveal	67	199	push	59	232	deliver	49
167	born	66	200	relate	59	233	engage	49
168	drive	66	201	acquire	58	234	handle	48
169	plan	66	202	attempt	58	235	occupy	48
170	study	66	203	refuse	57	236	bear	47
171	treat	66	204	afford	56	237	dominate	47
172	imagine	65	205	allow	56	238	knock	47
173	visit	65	206	approach	56	239	link	47
174	encourage	64	207	demonstrate	56	240	observe	47
175	pursue	64	208	launch	56	241	beat	46
176	supply	64	209	satisfy	56	242	contact	46
177	throw	64	210	speak	56	243	earn	46
178	answer	63	211	attack	55	244	limit	46
179	define	63	212	intend	55	245	conduct	45
180	gain	63	213	pull	55	246	divide	45
181	enter	62	214	sort	55	247	repeat	45
182	marry	62	215	state	55	248	commit	44
183	damage	61	216	ring	54	249	guess	44
184	note	61	217	test	54	250	justify	44
185	perform	61	218	impose	53	251	recommend	44
186	address	60	219	prepare	53	252	alter	43
187	arrange	60	220	attach	52	253	analyze	43
188	clear	60	221	experience	52	254	continue	43
189	finish	60	222	fit	52	255	feed	43
190	ignore	60	223	organize	52	256	illustrate	43
191	issue	60	224	own	52	257	mark	43
192	prove	60	225	retain	52	258	reject	43

259	assess	42	292	teach	37	325	match	31
260	attract	42	293	invite	36	326	register	31
261	phone	42	294	direct	35	327	stand	31
262	place	42	295	drop	35	328	sustain	31
263	secure	42	296	expose	35	329	bother	30
264	deny	41	297	extend	35	330	promote	30
265	fight	41	298	lift	35	331	shake	30
266	hand	41	299	shoot	35	332	waste	30
267	recall	41	300	absorb	34	333	welcome	30
268	resolve	41	301	begin	34	334	criticize	29
269	return	41	302	delay	34	335	estimate	29
270	threaten	41	303	detect	34	336	explore	29
271	combine	40	304	investigate	34	337	inform	29
272	emphasize	40	305	abandon	33	338	pretend	29
273	gather	40	306	accompany	33	339	refer	29
274	implement	40	307	clean	33	340	transfer	29
275	look	40	308	defend	33	341	calculate	28
276	block	39	309	drink	33	342	fulfill	28
277	derive	39	310	mind	33	343	fund	28
278	end	39	311	preserve	33	344	grow	28
279	generate	39	312	review	33	345	interpret	28
280	prefer	39	313	spread	33	346	operate	28
281	select	39	314	touch	33	347	promise	28
282	cross	38	315	charge	32	348	suspect	28
283	declare	38	316	interview	32	349	trace	28
284	demand	38	317	monitor	32	350	accuse	27
285	isolate	38	318	predict	32	351	confine	27
286	rule	38	319	quote	32	352	construct	27
287	blow	37	320	elect	31	353	cost	27
288	hate	37	321	entitle	31	354	deserve	27
289	press	37	322	force	31	355	head	27
290	store	37	323	imply	31	356	install	27
291	tackle	37	324	insist	31	357	invent	27

358	lack	27	391	print	24	424	undermine	22
359	list	27	392	question	24	425	weaken	22
360	paint	27	393	separate	24	426	advise	21
361	sing	27	394	steal	24	427	anticipate	21
362	surround	27	395	strengthen	24	428	borrow	21
363	view	27	396	transmit	24	429	burn	21
364	challenge	26	397	wash	24	430	chip	21
365	fear	26	398	accommodate	23	431	dismiss	21
366	incorporate	26	399	appoint	23	432	fold	21
367	mount	26	400	cook	23	433	live	21
368	suit	26	401	deposit	23	434	lock	21
369	sweep	26	402	dress	23	435	pose	21
370	switch	26	403	fix	23	436	reinforce	21
371	adjust	25	404	fly	23	437	restore	21
372	approve	25	405	hide	23	438	stimulate	21
373	bind	25	406	hurt	23	439	stress	21
374	book	25	407	locate	23	440	talk	21
375	capture	25	408	negotiate	23	441	trust	21
376	devote	25	409	possess	23	442	back	20
377	doubt	25	410	presume	23	443	bury	20
378	exclude	25	411	withdraw	23	444	confront	20
379	extract	25	412	arrest	22	445	connect	20
380	highlight	25	413	free	22	446	deal	20
381	renew	25	414	injure	22	447	disturb	20
382	resist	25	415	let	22	448	enhance	20
383	restrict	25	416	mix	22	449	fire	20
384	undertake	25	417	order	22	450	import	20
385	acknowledge	24	418	outline	22	451	initiate	20
386	conclude	24	419	request	22	452	name	20
387	consult	24	420	reverse	22	453	solve	20
388	distribute	24	421	settle	22	454	stick	20
389	exercise	24	422	train	22	455	unite	20
390	exploit	24	423	transport	22	456	blame	19

457	cancel	19
458	couple	19
459	defeat	19
460	dictate	19
461	envisage	19
462	finance	19
463	plant	19
464	process	19
465	regulate	19
466	score	19
467	specify	19
468	split	19
469	warn	19
470	clarify	18
471	decrease	18
472	deploy	18
473	deprive	18
474	devise	18
475	enforce	18
476	guarantee	18
477	impress	18
478	lend	18
479	overlook	18
480	perceive	18
481	plot	18
482	summarize	18
483	tie	18
484	wipe	18
485	adapt	17
486	await	17
487	count	17
488	educate	17
489	exceed	17

490	inspect	17
491	overcome	17
492	regret	17
493	scan	17
494	telephone	17
495	cast	16
496	celebrate	16
497	discharge	16
498	distinguish	16
499	edit	16
500	fancy	16
501	formulate	16
502	grant	16
503	judge	16
504	lower	16
505	manipulate	16
506	minimize	16
507	pack	16
508	reckon	16
509	recover	16
510	ride	16
511	submit	16
512	suspend	16
513	weigh	16
514	abolish	15
515	advocate	15
516	broadcast	15
517	chase	15
518	confuse	15
519	contemplate	15
520	copy	15
521	debate	15
522	govern	15

523	heat	15
524	illuminate	15
525	incur	15
526	invade	15
527	oppose	15
528	seize	15
529	sense	15
530	spot	15
531	trap	15
532	undergo	15
533	value	15
534	worry	15
535	correct	14
536	eliminate	14
537	equip	14
538	exhibit	14
539	export	14
540	focus	14
541	found	14
542	invest	14
543	liberate	14
544	modify	14
545	murder	14
546	portray	14
547	reserve	14
548	shape	14
549	shut	14
550	abuse	13
551	assemble	13
552	assert	13
553	assist	13
554	attribute	13
555	bend	13

付　録

556	bowl	13	589	chop	12	622	circulate	11
557	carve	13	590	classify	12	623	commission	11
558	characterize	13	591	complain	12	624	confer	11
559	delete	13	592	concede	12	625	decorate	11
560	drag	13	593	concentrate	12	626	dig	11
561	enable	13	594	condemn	12	627	encounter	11
562	equal	13	595	congratulate	12	628	execute	11
563	exchange	13	596	convert	12	629	forgive	11
564	exert	13	597	convey	12	630	guide	11
565	forward	13	598	defy	12	631	hesitate	11
566	foster	13	599	degrade	12	632	induce	11
567	inspire	13	600	dispute	12	633	inherit	11
568	insure	13	601	encode	12	634	inhibit	11
569	mobilize	13	602	enlarge	12	635	map	11
570	owe	13	603	escape	12	636	model	11
571	photograph	13	604	expand	12	637	neglect	11
572	post	13	605	favour	12	638	penetrate	11
573	punish	13	606	feature	12	639	precede	11
574	rebuild	13	607	hire	12	640	rent	11
575	regard	13	608	line	12	641	risk	11
576	reproduce	13	609	nominate	12	642	rub	11
577	resume	13	610	permit	12	643	tap	11
578	target	13	611	reward	12	644	tempt	11
579	terminate	13	612	spell	12	645	tidy	11
580	type	13	613	transform	12	646	tighten	11
581	underline	13	614	upset	12	647	track	11
582	update	13	615	witness	12	648	twist	11
583	utilize	13	616	activate	11	649	uphold	11
584	wake	13	617	administer	11	650	allocate	10
585	aid	12	618	allege	11	651	annoy	10
586	assign	12	619	amend	11	652	attain	10
587	authorise	12	620	balance	11	653	breach	10
588	bet	12	621	centre	11	654	code	10

655	command	10	688	surprise	10	721	power	9
656	comprehend	10	689	tear	10	722	practice	9
657	conceal	10	690	underestimate	10	723	project	9
658	damn	10	691	vote	10	724	recount	9
659	date	10	692	wave	10	725	reform	9
660	drill	10	693	whip	10	726	regain	9
661	embrace	10	694	accomplish	9	727	rehearse	9
662	erode	10	695	advance	9	728	respect	9
663	excuse	10	696	arouse	9	729	restrain	9
664	file	10	697	award	9	730	scatter	9
665	flick	10	698	boost	9	731	second	9
666	hang	10	699	care	9	732	sit	9
667	infer	10	700	compile	9	733	smash	9
668	inhabit	10	701	compose	9	734	spare	9
669	plug	10	702	contribute	9	735	stage	9
670	poke	10	703	convict	9	736	strive	9
671	position	10	704	depend	9	737	suppress	9
672	pour	10	705	discount	9	738	survive	9
673	prompt	10	706	discourage	9	739	swear	9
674	provoke	10	707	disguise	9	740	swing	9
675	purchase	10	708	dislike	9	741	translate	9
676	re-create	10	709	divorce	9	742	travel	9
677	recruit	10	710	ease	9	743	trigger	9
678	repair	10	711	effect	9	744	tune	9
679	revive	10	712	greet	9	745	undo	9
680	roll	10	713	hamper	9	746	urge	9
681	sacrifice	10	714	house	9	747	voice	9
682	signify	10	715	inflict	9	748	admire	8
683	simulate	10	716	kick	9	749	advertise	8
684	slice	10	717	light	9	750	climb	8
685	squeeze	10	718	load	9	751	conquer	8
686	strip	10	719	manufacture	9	752	correlate	8
687	sum	10	720	poison	9	753	credit	8

754	cure	8	787	refine	8	820	deduce	7
755	decline	8	788	refit	8	821	defer	7
756	desire	8	789	relieve	8	822	despise	7
757	detach	8	790	resemble	8	823	deter	7
758	detail	8	791	root	8	824	diminish	7
759	disappoint	8	792	screen	8	825	disregard	7
760	disclose	8	793	seduce	8	826	draft	7
761	displace	8	794	speed	8	827	endorse	7
762	distort	8	795	stretch	8	828	extinguish	7
763	double	8	796	structure	8	829	facilitate	7
764	dry	8	797	succeed	8	830	fail	7
765	echo	8	798	sue	8	831	filter	7
766	embarrass	8	799	surrender	8	832	grab	7
767	emit	8	800	swallow	8	833	honour	7
768	enact	8	801	tape	8	834	hook	7
769	endure	8	802	tuck	8	835	impart	7
770	entertain	8	803	vary	8	836	insert	7
771	evaluate	8	804	wait	8	837	insult	7
772	evoke	8	805	widen	8	838	interest	7
773	fuel	8	806	accelerate	7	839	interrupt	7
774	harm	8	807	alienate	7	840	invoke	7
775	hoist	8	808	avert	7	841	license	7
776	milk	8	809	ban	7	842	mask	7
777	narrow	8	810	benefit	7	843	master	7
778	net	8	811	betray	7	844	merge	7
779	overwhelm	8	812	cf.	7	845	overtake	7
780	pilot	8	813	chart	7	846	park	7
781	pitch	8	814	commend	7	847	plead	7
782	plough	8	815	conceive	7	848	please	7
783	police	8	816	consume	7	849	postpone	7
784	pump	8	817	contrast	7	850	praise	7
785	radiate	8	818	convince	7	851	pray	7
786	redefine	8	819	crush	7	852	prescribe	7

853	prosecute	7	886	wrap	7	919	endanger	6
854	reassure	7	887	align	6	920	entail	6
855	reconsider	7	888	amaze	6	921	evacuate	6
856	re-establish	7	889	anger	6	922	exacerbate	6
857	retrieve	7	890	ascertain	6	923	exaggerate	6
858	revise	7	891	augment	6	924	exemplify	6
859	rid	7	892	beg	6	925	expend	6
860	ruin	7	893	bite	6	926	flood	6
861	schedule	7	894	bless	6	927	foresee	6
862	scrap	7	895	brush	6	928	forge	6
863	scrape	7	896	chew	6	929	freeze	6
864	screw	7	897	cite	6	930	frighten	6
865	shock	7	898	clip	6	931	group	6
866	signal	7	899	clothe	6	932	guard	6
867	simplify	7	900	communicate	6	933	halt	6
868	slacken	7	901	complicate	6	934	harbour	6
869	spill	7	902	confess	6	935	incline	6
870	square	7	903	conjure	6	936	innervate	6
871	stir	7	904	constrain	6	937	intrigue	6
872	subject	7	905	contaminate	6	938	jump	6
873	summon	7	906	coordinate	6	939	levy	6
874	tabled	7	907	counter	6	940	mimic	6
875	time	7	908	cross-examine	6	941	obey	6
876	tolerate	7	909	cube	6	942	obscure	6
877	top	7	910	demolish	6	943	offend	6
878	torture	7	911	depict	6	944	oust	6
879	trim	7	912	differentiate	6	945	persuade	6
880	trouble	7	913	digitise	6	946	pin	6
881	underpin	7	914	discard	6	947	pledge	6
882	walk	7	915	discredit	6	948	ponder	6
883	warm	7	916	divert	6	949	privatise	6
884	withhold	7	917	document	6	950	pronounce	6
885	worship	7	918	dump	6	951	publicise	6

952	rape	6	985	abstract	5	1018	farm	5
953	readmit	6	986	air	5	1019	fax	5
954	redistribute	6	987	average	5	1020	fine	5
955	reinstate	6	988	bang	5	1021	fry	5
956	relish	6	989	border	5	1022	gag	5
957	reopen	6	990	bore	5	1023	grasp	5
958	round	6	991	bound	5	1024	grip	5
959	saw	6	992	breathe	5	1025	hammer	5
960	seal	6	993	brief	5	1026	harness	5
961	sentence	6	994	calm	5	1027	hassle	5
962	shed	6	995	canonize	5	1028	horrify	5
963	shrug	6	996	chuck	5	1029	hug	5
964	slaughter	6	997	coin	5	1030	impede	5
965	slide	6	998	combat	5	1031	inject	5
966	slip	6	999	comfort	5	1032	inquire	5
967	smell	6	1000	commence	5	1033	integrate	5
968	soak	6	1001	compromise	5	1034	intercept	5
969	sponsor	6	1002	conserve	5	1035	kiss	5
970	spray	6	1003	contest	5	1036	label	5
971	squash	6	1004	contradict	5	1037	land	5
972	sting	6	1005	depress	5	1038	loot	5
973	synthesize	6	1006	despatch	5	1039	man	5
974	tip	6	1007	dismantle	5	1040	mend	5
975	trade	6	1008	disperse	5	1041	misjudge	5
976	transcribe	6	1009	dissolve	5	1042	mislead	5
977	underlie	6	1010	drown	5	1043	motivate	5
978	unveil	6	1011	encompass	5	1044	necessitate	5
979	volunteer	6	1012	endeavour	5	1045	obstruct	5
980	wage	6	1013	equate	5	1046	override	5
981	wind	6	1014	eradicate	5	1047	overrun	5
982	wound	6	1015	erect	5	1048	overturn	5
983	yield	6	1016	excite	5	1049	oxidize	5
984	<unclear-word>	5	1017	expel	5	1050	pave	5

1051	pervert	5	1084	unleash	5	1117	deduct	4
1052	photocopy	5	1085	utter	5	1118	deepen	4
1053	pinpoint	5	1086	wield	5	1119	denounce	4
1054	pluck	5	1087	withstand	5	1120	deplete	4
1055	pressure	5	1088	abort	4	1121	designate	4
1056	program	5	1089	access	4	1122	detain	4
1057	ratify	5	1090	account	4	1123	devastate	4
1058	reconcile	5	1091	addict	4	1124	devour	4
1059	reconstruct	5	1092	adduce	4	1125	dial	4
1060	relax	5	1093	adore	4	1126	discipline	4
1061	repay	5	1094	articulate	4	1127	dispatch	4
1062	repeal	5	1095	ascribe	4	1128	disrupt	4
1063	repel	5	1096	awaken	4	1129	donate	4
1064	reprint	5	1097	blend	4	1130	down	4
1065	satirise	5	1098	boss	4	1131	duplicate	4
1066	scratch	5	1099	breed	4	1132	edge	4
1067	search	5	1100	bribe	4	1133	elevate	4
1068	service	5	1101	bud	4	1134	embed	4
1069	sever	5	1102	bypass	4	1135	embody	4
1070	shuffle	5	1103	calibrate	4	1136	empty	4
1071	sink	5	1104	cease	4	1137	enrich	4
1072	site	5	1105	chair	4	1138	entrust	4
1073	situate	5	1106	coach	4	1139	envelop	4
1074	sketch	5	1107	colonize	4	1140	envy	4
1075	smooth	5	1108	comment	4	1141	equalize	4
1076	snap	5	1109	compensate	4	1142	erase	4
1077	steady	5	1110	consolidate	4	1143	evolve	4
1078	stifle	5	1111	contract	4	1144	exile	4
1079	subvert	5	1112	crown	4	1145	extrude	4
1080	topple	5	1113	curb	4	1146	fascinate	4
1081	toss	5	1114	curl	4	1147	float	4
1082	tour	5	1115	decree	4	1148	forecast	4
1083	transcend	5	1116	dedicate	4	1149	fudge	4

1150	further	4
1151	gate	4
1152	gear	4
1153	ground	4
1154	haul	4
1155	haunt	4
1156	heal	4
1157	heighten	4
1158	hunt	4
1159	hypothesize	4
1160	infect	4
1161	institute	4
1162	intensify	4
1163	inundate	4
1164	kidnap	4
1165	liken	4
1166	magnify	4
1167	manifest	4
1168	maximize	4
1169	mince	4
1170	mirror	4
1171	nick	4
1172	notify	4
1173	overplay	4
1174	parallel	4
1175	penalise	4
1176	preclude	4
1177	preoccupy	4
1178	price	4
1179	proclaim	4
1180	prop	4
1181	punch	4
1182	purport	4

1183	quicken	4
1184	rate	4
1185	rationalize	4
1186	rearrange	4
1187	recite	4
1188	recycle	4
1189	refute	4
1190	relie	4
1191	relocate	4
1192	remark	4
1193	reorganize	4
1194	reply	4
1195	repress	4
1196	rescue	4
1197	resent	4
1198	resign	4
1199	rest	4
1200	restart	4
1201	rip	4
1202	rock	4
1203	rush	4
1204	scoop	4
1205	secrete	4
1206	shave	4
1207	shine	4
1208	slam	4
1209	slap	4
1210	smear	4
1211	smuggle	4
1212	snatch	4
1213	span	4
1214	stab	4
1215	stack	4

1216	strain	4
1217	strew	4
1218	stroke	4
1219	struggle	4
1220	suck	4
1221	superimpose	4
1222	supervise	4
1223	survey	4
1224	swap	4
1225	symbolize	4
1226	temper	4
1227	thwart	4
1228	tick	4
1229	total	4
1230	trick	4
1231	uncover	4
1232	verify	4
1233	violate	4
1234	weather	4
1235	abduct	3
1236	accentuate	3
1237	accumulate	3
1238	acquaint	3
1239	act	3
1240	alert	3
1241	amplify	3
1242	amuse	3
1243	ape	3
1244	appease	3
1245	arm	3
1246	assassinate	3
1247	assuage	3
1248	assure	3

1249	astonish	3
1250	astound	3
1251	attenuate	3
1252	audition	3
1253	bash	3
1254	belittle	3
1255	bestow	3
1256	better	3
1257	blackmail	3
1258	blunt	3
1259	boast	3
1260	bomb	3
1261	bombard	3
1262	bottle	3
1263	bounce	3
1264	brave	3
1265	bunny	3
1266	buttress	3
1267	canvass	3
1268	cash	3
1269	castigate	3
1270	categorize	3
1271	cement	3
1272	charm	3
1273	cheat	3
1274	cherish	3
1275	chest	3
1276	churn	3
1277	circumvent	3
1278	cleave	3
1279	clench	3
1280	clock	3
1281	clutch	3

1282	coat	3
1283	cobble	3
1284	colour	3
1285	compel	3
1286	compost	3
1287	condition	3
1288	confiscate	3
1289	contend	3
1290	convene	3
1291	cough	3
1292	countenance	3
1293	crack	3
1294	cram	3
1295	crucify	3
1296	cultivate	3
1297	dance	3
1298	daresay	3
1299	decode	3
1300	deflect	3
1301	deform	3
1302	delegate	3
1303	delight	3
1304	denervate	3
1305	denote	3
1306	destabilise	3
1307	diagnose	3
1308	die	3
1309	diffuse	3
1310	dip	3
1311	disallow	3
1312	dispel	3
1313	dispose	3
1314	distance	3

1315	drain	3
1316	dream	3
1317	dye	3
1318	elicit	3
1319	emulate	3
1320	endow	3
1321	energize	3
1322	engulf	3
1323	enshrine	3
1324	eschew	3
1325	excavate	3
1326	except	3
1327	excrete	3
1328	exempt	3
1329	exhaust	3
1330	explode	3
1331	extol	3
1332	extricate	3
1333	fell	4
1334	festoon	3
1335	fetch	3
1336	field	3
1337	film	3
1338	flash	3
1339	flatten	3
1340	flatter	3
1341	flout	3
1342	flush	3
1343	forbid	3
1344	formalise	3
1345	foul	3
1346	furnish	3
1347	gauge	3

1348	gloss	3	1381	moisten	3	1414	redo	3
1349	glue	3	1382	mouth	3	1415	redress	3
1350	graze	3	1383	multiply	3	1416	refurbish	3
1351	grind	3	1384	nod	3	1417	regenerate	3
1352	hack	3	1385	nudge	3	1418	reinvest	3
1353	handicap	3	1386	obliterate	3	1419	reissue	3
1354	herd	3	1387	obsess	3	1420	reiterate	3
1355	hijack	3	1388	offset	3	1421	relay	3
1356	humiliate	3	1389	overhear	3	1422	rend	3
1357	hypnotise	3	1390	overlie	3	1423	reproach	3
1358	impair	3	1391	pace	3	1424	research	3
1359	impound	3	1392	parade	3	1425	reset	3
1360	imprison	3	1393	paralyse	3	1426	retake	3
1361	inaugurate	3	1394	pile	3	1427	revisit	3
1362	inculcate	3	1395	pioneer	3	1428	revitalize	3
1363	intersperse	3	1396	plunge	3	1429	rework	3
1364	jam	3	1397	poise	3	1430	rewrite	3
1365	jar	3	1398	polish	3	1431	right	3
1366	jeopardise	3	1399	pop	3	1432	roar	3
1367	lace	3	1400	popularize	3	1433	rob	3
1368	lade	3	1401	preach	3	1434	rot	3
1369	lavish	3	1402	precipitate	3	1435	rotate	3
1370	level	3	1403	prime	3	1436	safeguard	3
1371	lever	3	1404	propel	3	1437	salute	3
1372	lodge	3	1405	puncture	3	1438	salvage	3
1373	log	3	1406	purée	3	1439	scale	3
1374	long	3	1407	qualify	3	1440	scour	3
1375	loosen	3	1408	rattle	3	1441	scrub	3
1376	melt	3	1409	react	3	1442	sew	3
1377	mesmerise	3	1410	reassert	3	1443	shade	3
1378	mess	3	1411	recheck	3	1444	shatter	3
1379	mine	3	1412	recollect	3	1445	shell	3
1380	misread	3	1413	redeem	3	1446	shift	3

1447	ship	3
1448	shop	3
1449	shove	3
1450	slag	3
1451	slash	3
1452	slow	3
1453	smother	3
1454	snog	3
1455	soften	3
1456	sound	3
1457	space	3
1458	spike	3
1459	spin	3
1460	spur	3
1461	stabilise	3
1462	steer	3
1463	straddle	3
1464	straighten	3
1465	stuff	3
1466	subdivide	3
1467	subsidise	3
1468	supplement	3
1469	surmount	3
1470	swamp	3
1471	terrify	3
1472	thread	3
1473	thrust	3
1474	toast	3
1475	trail	3
1476	traumatise	3
1477	tread	3
1478	treble	3
1479	unify	3

1480	unload	3
1481	unpack	3
1482	upgrade	3
1483	vow	3
1484	waive	3
1485	ward	3
1486	warrant	3
1487	water	3
1488	weave	3
1489	wet	3
1490	wizz	3
1491	wreck	3
1492	acquit	2
1493	adjoin	2
1494	adjourn	2
1495	aerate	2
1496	affirm	2
1497	afflict	2
1498	airlift	2
1499	alleviate	2
1500	ally	2
1501	ameliorate	2
1502	amputate	2
1503	angle	2
1504	annihilate	2
1505	applaud	2
1506	appropriate	2
1507	approximate	2
1508	assault	2
1509	assimilate	2
1510	audit	2
1511	b	2
1512	baffle	2

1513	bandage	2
1514	banish	2
1515	bankroll	2
1516	bar	2
1517	bemuse	2
1518	bequeath	2
1519	bill	2
1520	blackleg	2
1521	blanket	2
1522	blast	2
1523	blot	2
1524	bluff	2
1525	board	2
1526	bolt	2
1527	bond	2
1528	brace	2
1529	bracket	2
1530	brick	2
1531	bridge	2
1532	broker	2
1533	brown	2
1534	bruise	2
1535	buffer	2
1536	bulldoze	2
1537	bung	2
1538	bungle	2
1539	burden	2
1540	button	2
1541	caricature	2
1542	catalogue	2
1543	caution	2
1544	censor	2
1545	centralise	2

1546	certify	2	1579	curse	2	1612	dispossess	2
1547	champion	2	1580	curtail	2	1613	disprove	2
1548	channel	2	1581	cycle	2	1614	dissipate	2
1549	chant	2	1582	dab	2	1615	dissociate	2
1550	chat	2	1583	darken	2	1616	distract	2
1551	cheer	2	1584	dash	2	1617	ditch	2
1552	chisel	2	1585	deassign	2	1618	diversify	2
1553	choke	2	1586	deceive	2	1619	dodge	2
1554	circumscribe	2	1587	decipher	2	1620	don	2
1555	clamp	2	1588	defuse	2	1621	doom	2
1556	class	2	1589	delineate	2	1622	double-cross	2
1557	clinch	2	1590	delude	2	1623	drum	2
1558	clog	2	1591	denigrate	2	1624	dust	2
1559	cock	2	1592	dent	2	1625	efface	2
1560	commemorate	2	1593	denude	2	1626	elongate	2
1561	complement	2	1594	deport	2	1627	elucidate	2
1562	complie	2	1595	deride	2	1628	elude	2
1563	compound	2	1596	desert	2	1629	emasculate	2
1564	compute	2	1597	detest	2	1630	embellish	2
1565	conceptualize	2	1598	dethrone	2	1631	encapsulate	2
1566	concordance	2	1599	devalue	2	1632	enliven	2
1567	concrete	2	1600	devolve	2	1633	enroll	2
1568	condone	2	1601	digest	2	1634	enthuse	2
1569	configure	2	1602	dilute	2	1635	entwine	2
1570	consign	2	1603	dim	2	1636	espouse	2
1571	constrict	2	1604	direct-mail	2	1637	etch	2
1572	construe	2	1605	discern	2	1638	evade	2
1573	contrive	2	1606	discomfit	2	1639	evict	2
1574	counteract	2	1607	disengage	2	1640	excommunicate	2
1575	court	2	1608	disk	2	1641	exorcise	2
1576	cradle	2	1609	dislocate	2	1642	expound	2
1577	crowd	2	1610	dismember	2	1643	eye	2
1578	cup	2	1611	disobey	2	1644	fabricate	2

1645	fake	2		1678	homogenise	2		1711	mangle	2
1646	fashion	2		1679	hoover	2		1712	manoeuvre	2
1647	fasten	2		1680	hospitalise	2		1713	mass produce	2
1648	feign	2		1681	host	2		1714	mastermind	2
1649	ferret	2		1682	hurl	2		1715	merit	2
1650	ferry	2		1683	imitate	2		1716	metabolise	2
1651	fertilize	2		1684	immerse	2		1717	misinterpret	2
1652	fiddle	2		1685	implicate	2		1718	mistake	2
1653	figure	2		1686	individualise	2		1719	misunderstand	2
1654	finalize	2		1687	innovate	2		1720	modulate	2
1655	fish	2		1688	instil	2		1721	mountain fold	2
1656	flip	2		1689	instruct	2		1722	mourn	2
1657	forewarn	2		1690	insulate	2		1723	muster	2
1658	forsake	2		1691	intimidate	2		1724	mystify	2
1659	fracture	2		1692	intone	2		1725	nationalize	2
1660	frame	2		1693	intoxicate	2		1726	neutralize	2
1661	front	2		1694	inure	2		1727	nurse	2
1662	frustrate	2		1695	invalidate	2		1728	oblige	2
1663	galvanise	2		1696	irritate	2		1729	obviate	2
1664	glimpse	2		1697	jail	2		1730	opt	2
1665	go	2		1698	jettison	2		1731	outlaw	2
1666	grade	2		1699	jolt	2		1732	outnumber	2
1667	graft	2		1700	juxtapose	2		1733	output	2
1668	gut	2		1701	kickstart	2		1734	out-run	2
1669	harass	2		1702	kindle	2		1735	outstrip	2
1670	harden	2		1703	lament	2		1736	outweigh	2
1671	harvest	2		1704	lasso	2		1737	overdo	2
1672	hasten	2		1705	last	2		1738	overlap	2
1673	have rather	2		1706	lease	2		1739	overlay	2
1674	heed	2		1707	legislate	2		1740	overstate	2
1675	herald	2		1708	litter	2		1741	overthrow	2
1676	hinder	2		1709	lob	2		1742	palm	2
1677	hint	2		1710	lure	2		1743	pardon	2

1744	parry	2	1777	purify	2	1810	renovate	2
1745	part	2	1778	quantify	2	1811	republish	2
1746	paste	2	1779	quarter	2	1812	repudiate	2
1747	patent	2	1780	query	2	1813	retire	2
1748	peel	2	1781	randomise	2	1814	revamp	2
1749	perfect	2	1782	range	2	1815	revere	2
1750	perpetrate	2	1783	rate cap	2	1816	riddle	2
1751	perpetuate	2	1784	re-absorb	2	1817	rival	2
1752	persecute	2	1785	ready	2	1818	rocket	2
1753	personify	2	1786	reaffirm	2	1819	romanize	2
1754	pester	2	1787	re-allocate	2	1820	rouse	2
1755	phrase	2	1788	re-analyse	2	1821	rout	2
1756	picture	2	1789	reassess	2	1822	rubbish	2
1757	placate	2	1790	reborn	2	1823	rupture	2
1758	ply	2	1791	rebuke	2	1824	sack	2
1759	pool	2	1792	recalculate	2	1825	sadden	2
1760	populate	2	1793	recapture	2	1826	sanction	2
1761	predate	2	1794	reclaim	2	1827	scare	2
1762	preface	2	1795	recode	2	1828	segregate	2
1763	prefigure	2	1796	re-crease	2	1829	sharpen	2
1764	preprogram	2	1797	redecorate	2	1830	shelve	2
1765	preset	2	1798	redeliver	2	1831	shield	2
1766	presuppose	2	1799	redirect	2	1832	shoulder	2
1767	prevail	2	1800	re-enter	2	1833	shout	2
1768	pride	2	1801	refigure	2	1834	shrink	2
1769	procure	2	1802	reimburse	2	1835	shun	2
1770	prohibit	2	1803	re-join	2	1836	silence	2
1771	prolong	2	1804	rejuvenate	2	1837	silt	2
1772	promulgate	2	1805	relegate	2	1838	skip	2
1773	propagate	2	1806	relicense	2	1839	slate	2
1774	prophesy	2	1807	relinquish	2	1840	sleep	2
1775	psyche	2	1808	remind	2	1841	sow	2
1776	punctuate	2	1809	render	2	1842	spear	2

1843	speculate	2
1844	spit	2
1845	sport	2
1846	spurn	2
1847	squander	2
1848	staff	2
1849	stamp	2
1850	standardize	2
1851	star	2
1852	starve	2
1853	steam roll	2
1854	stem	2
1855	stock	2
1856	stockpile	2
1857	strand	2
1858	string	2
1859	stun	2
1860	subscribe	2
1861	substantiate	2
1862	subsume	2
1863	suffocate	2
1864	supersede	2
1865	suss	2
1866	swat	2
1867	sweeten	2
1868	swell	2
1869	tar	2
1870	taste	2
1871	tax	2
1872	tease	2
1873	terrorise	2
1874	tickle	2
1875	tilt	2

1876	tire	2
1877	torch	2
1878	tow	2
1879	trample	2
1880	transgress	2
1881	triple	2
1882	twiddle	2
1883	underscore	2
1884	underwrite	2
1885	unravel	2
1886	unscramble	2
1887	untie	2
1888	up	2
1889	validate	2
1890	verbalise	2
1891	vet	2
1892	wax	2
1893	weep	2
1894	wheel	2
1895	will	2
1896	woo	2
1897	wreak	2
1898	wrench	2
1899	=	1
1900	abbreviate	1
1901	abet	1
1902	abhor	1
1903	abide	1
1904	absolve	1
1905	accession	1
1906	acclaim	1
1907	accredit	1
1908	accrete	1

1909	action	1
1910	ad lib	1
1911	adorn	1
1912	affiliate	1
1913	aggravate	1
1914	allay	1
1915	allude	1
1916	amass	1
1917	anchor	1
1918	annex	1
1919	antagonise	1
1920	appear	1
1921	append	1
1922	apportion	1
1923	appose	1
1924	appraise	1
1925	apprehend	1
1926	arbitrate	1
1927	archive	1
1928	armour	1
1929	article	1
1930	aspirate	1
1931	assail	1
1932	attest	1
1933	attune	1
1934	auction	1
1935	authenticate	1
1936	author	1
1937	automate	1
1938	avail	1
1939	avoid/minimise	1
1940	avow	1
1941	ax	1

1942	backdate	1	1975	betoken	1	2008	cart	1
1943	backfill	1	1976	bide	1	2009	catalyse	1
1944	badger	1	1977	bisect	1	2010	cater	1
1945	bag	1	1978	black	1	2011	cauterise	1
1946	bail	1	1979	blaze	1	2012	chain	1
1947	bake	1	1980	bleach	1	2013	chance	1
1948	bamboozle	1	1981	bleat	1	2014	chevy	1
1949	bandy	1	1982	bleed	1	2015	chill	1
1950	bank	1	1983	bleep	1	2016	chisel	1
1951	bankrupt	1	1984	blindfold	1	2017	christen	1
1952	barbecue	1	1985	blitz	1	2018	chubb lock	1
1953	bare	1	1986	boil	1	2019	clasp	1
1954	barricade	1	1987	boot	1	2020	clobber	1
1955	bathe	1	1988	boycott	1	2021	codify	1
1956	batten	1	1989	brand	1	2022	coerce	1
1957	batter	1	1990	breast-feed	1	2023	collide	1
1958	beach	1	1991	breath-test	1	2024	comb	1
1959	beckon	1	1992	brighten	1	2025	come	1
1960	become	1	1993	broach	1	2026	commandeer	1
1961	bedevil	1	1994	broaden	1	2027	comminute	1
1962	befit	1	1995	brook	1	2028	compress	1
1963	beget	1	1996	bubble	1	2029	comprise	1
1964	behead	1	1997	bunch	1	2030	concoct	1
1965	behold	1	1998	bundle	1	2031	concuss	1
1966	belie	1	1999	burgle	1	2032	condense	1
1967	belove	1	2000	bus	1	2033	conflate	1
1968	belt	1	2001	butcher	1	2034	confound	1
1969	berate	1	2002	butt weld	1	2035	conjour	1
1970	bereave	1	2003	butter	1	2036	conjugate	1
1971	berth	1	2004	cajole	1	2037	consecrate	1
1972	beset	1	2005	camouflage	1	2038	contextualise	1
1973	besiege	1	2006	campaign	1	2039	contravene	1
1974	betide	1	2007	carpet	1	2040	controvert	1

2041	cool	1		2074	deign	1		2107	disparage	1
2042	cope	1		2075	de-localise	1		2108	disqualify	1
2043	cordon	1		2076	deluge	1		2109	disseminate	1
2044	corner	1		2077	demonise	1		2110	distress	1
2045	corrupt	1		2078	denationalize	1		2111	distrust	1
2046	couch	1		2079	depart	1		2112	dog	1
2047	counsel	1		2080	deplore	1		2113	dole	1
2048	counterpoint	1		2081	depose	1		2114	dope	1
2049	countersign	1		2082	de-regulate	1		2115	downgrade	1
2050	co-write	1		2083	descale	1		2116	downplay	1
2051	crash	1		2084	descend	1		2117	dramatise	1
2052	crave	1		2085	despoil	1		2118	drape	1
2053	cripple	1		2086	destine	1		2119	dread	1
2054	cross-reference	1		2087	detoxify	1		2120	drench	1
2055	cross-section	1		2088	ding	1		2121	dumbfound	1
2056	crust	1		2089	dink	1		2122	earmark	1
2057	cry	1		2090	diode OR	1		2123	eclipse	1
2058	culminate	1		2091	disable	1		2124	economise	1
2059	custom-build	1		2092	disassociate	1		2125	eject	1
2060	damp	1		2093	disavow	1		2126	elaborate	1
2061	dangle	1		2094	disconcert	1		2127	elbow	1
2062	dazzle	1		2095	disconnect	1		2128	electrocute	1
2063	deaden	1		2096	discriminate	1		2129	embark	1
2064	debar	1		2097	disenfranchise	1		2130	embroider	1
2065	debase	1		2098	disentangle	1		2131	embroil	1
2066	debride	1		2099	disfigure	1		2132	emerse	1
2067	debrief	1		2100	disgust	1		2133	emphasize/reiterate	1
2068	debug	1		2101	dish	1		2134	emplace	1
2069	decentralise	1		2102	dishearten	1		2135	encamp	1
2070	declaim	1		2103	dishonour	1		2136	encase	1
2071	deep-freeze	1		2104	disinherit	1		2137	enchant	1
2072	deflate	1		2105	disintegrate	1		2138	encircle	1
2073	defrost	1		2106	disjoin	1		2139	encumber	1

2140	endear	1	2173	flank	1	2206	gird	1
2141	enfeeble	1	2174	flaunt	1	2207	glamorize	1
2142	enfranchise	1	2175	fledge	1	2208	glide	1
2143	engender	1	2176	flee	1	2209	gobble	1
2144	engineer	1	2177	flesh	1	2210	gold coat	1
2145	engrave	1	2178	flex	1	2211	gore	1
2146	enthral	1	2179	flog	1	2212	gratify	1
2147	entice	1	2180	flummox	1	2213	grill	1
2148	entrench	1	2181	fob	1	2214	gush	1
2149	envision	1	2182	foist	1	2215	halve	1
2150	escort	1	2183	foment	1	2216	hand rear	1
2151	esteem	1	2184	foot	1	2217	harangue	1
2152	evangelise	1	2185	force-feed	1	2218	hardwire	1
2153	evidence	1	2186	forfeit	1	2219	hatch	1
2154	evince	1	2187	fork	1	2220	heave	1
2155	excise	1	2188	fortify	1	2221	hive	1
2156	exclaim	1	2189	fossilize	1	2222	hoard	1
2157	excoriate	1	2190	fox	1	2223	hound	1
2158	exit	1	2191	frequent	1	2224	huddle	1
2159	expedite	1	2192	freshen	1	2225	humble	1
2160	explicate	1	2193	fringe	1	2226	hump	1
2161	expunge	1	2194	fuck	1	2227	hurtle	1
2162	exterminate	1	2195	fuse	1	2228	hustle	1
2163	extort	1	2196	gainsay	1	2229	hydrolyse	1
2164	extradite	1	2197	gall	1	2230	hype	1
2165	fan	1	2198	gap	1	2231	ignite	1
2166	fast-track	1	2199	gas	1	2232	imbue	1
2167	father	1	2200	gasp	1	2233	immortalize	1
2168	faze	1	2201	gatecrash	1	2234	impale	1
2169	fence	1	2202	generalize	1	2235	implant	1
2170	fine-tune	1	2203	gentle	1	2236	impregnant	1
2171	flag	1	2204	ghost-write	1	2237	improvise	1
2172	flagellate	1	2205	ginger	1	2238	impugn	1

2239	incarcerate	1
2240	incise	1
2241	incriminate	1
2242	index	1
2243	industrialise	1
2244	infatuate	1
2245	infest	1
2246	infill	1
2247	inflate	1
2248	infuriate	1
2249	ingest	1
2250	inhale	1
2251	inlay	1
2252	input	1
2253	inset	1
2254	inside edge	1
2255	instigate	1
2256	institutionalize	1
2257	interconnect	1
2258	intersect	1
2259	interweave	1
2260	intimate	1
2261	invert	1
2262	invoice	1
2263	iron	1
2264	iterate	1
2265	jerk	1
2266	joggle	1
2267	joke	1
2268	jot	1
2269	junk	1
2270	kirtle	1
2271	kit	1

2272	knacker	1
2273	knead	1
2274	knight	1
2275	knit	1
2276	lap	1
2277	laugh	1
2278	leach	1
2279	leak	1
2280	lean	1
2281	leapfrog	1
2282	legalise	1
2283	legitimate	1
2284	legitimize	1
2285	lengthen	1
2286	liberalize	1
2287	lick	1
2288	lie1	1
2289	lithify	1
2290	loathe	1
2291	localise	1
2292	loft	1
2293	loose	1
2294	lop	1
2295	lord	1
2296	lug	1
2297	lump	1
2298	magnetize	1
2299	mandate	1
2300	manhandle	1
2301	mar	1
2302	marginalise	1
2303	market	1
2304	marshal	1

2305	mass mobilise	1
2306	massacre	1
2307	massage	1
2308	mat	1
2309	matter	1
2310	mature	1
2311	means-test	1
2312	mediate	1
2313	mesh	1
2314	message	1
2315	microwave	1
2316	mime	1
2317	mishear	1
2318	mislay	1
2319	misquote	1
2320	misremember	1
2321	misrepresent	1
2322	misspell	1
2323	misuse	1
2324	mob	1
2325	moderate	1
2326	modernise	1
2327	molest	1
2328	mould	1
2329	muck	1
2330	muddle	1
2331	muddy	1
2332	multiplex	1
2333	mumble	1
2334	mummify	1
2335	mutate	1
2336	mutilate	1
2337	mutter	1

2338	mythologize	1	2371	overestimate	1	2404	pet	1
2339	nail	1	2372	overindulge	1	2405	phagocytose	1
2340	near	1	2373	overlap	1	2406	phase	1
2341	negate	1	2374	overload	1	2407	pierce	1
2342	nestle	1	2375	over-mince	1	2408	pillage	1
2343	nobble	1	2376	over-record	1	2409	pinch	1
2344	normalize	1	2377	overrule	1	2410	piss	1
2345	notch	1	2378	oversee	1	2411	plait	1
2346	nourish	1	2379	overshadow	1	2412	plaster	1
2347	novate	1	2380	overshoot	1	2413	pleat	1
2348	occasion	1	2381	overstay	1	2414	plonk	1
2349	ok	1	2382	over-step	1	2415	plumb	1
2350	omit	1	2383	overview	1	2416	plunder	1
2351	oppress	1	2384	overwork	1	2417	poach	1
2352	optimize	1	2385	pacify	1	2418	poeticize	1
2353	OR	1	2386	package	1	2419	poll tax cap	1
2354	orbit	1	2387	pad	1	2420	pollute	1
2355	orchestrate	1	2388	paginate	1	2421	posit	1
2356	ordain	1	2389	pamper	1	2422	postulate	1
2357	orientate	1	2390	paper	1	2423	pot	1
2358	outbid	1	2391	partner	1	2424	potentiate	1
2359	outdo	1	2392	pat	1	2425	pound	1
2360	outgrow	1	2393	patch	1	2426	prearrange	1
2361	outlive	1	2394	patrol	1	2427	pre-cook	1
2362	outmode	1	2395	pedestrianise	1	2428	predicate	1
2363	outperform	1	2396	peg	1	2429	prejudge	1
2364	outplay	1	2397	pen	1	2430	prejudice	1
2365	outshine	1	2398	pencil	1	2431	premise	1
2366	outside reverse	1	2399	people	1	2432	pre-select	1
2367	outsprint	1	2400	pepper	1	2433	pre-sort	1
2368	overawe	1	2401	perish	1	2434	press-gang	1
2369	overburden	1	2402	perturb	1	2435	preview	1
2370	overdramatize	1	2403	pervade	1	2436	prize	1

2437	probe	1	2470	rear	1	2503	reign	1
2438	procedurise	1	2471	reason	1	2504	reincarnate	1
2439	proceed	1	2472	rebody	1	2505	reintegrate	1
2440	procreate	1	2473	rebuff	1	2506	re-introduce	1
2441	proffer	1	2474	rebut	1	2507	relive	1
2442	profile	1	2475	recharge	1	2508	remeasure	1
2443	proof-read	1	2476	recirculate	1	2509	renarrate	1
2444	proscribe	1	2477	recommence	1	2510	renationalise	1
2445	prostrate	1	2478	re-copy	1	2511	renounce	1
2446	protest	1	2479	rectify	1	2512	reorder	1
2447	prune	1	2480	redeploy	1	2513	repackage	1
2448	purge	1	2481	redesign	1	2514	repatriate	1
2449	putrefiy	1	2482	redevelop	1	2515	replaster	1
2450	quantitate	1	2483	rediscover	1	2516	replenish	1
2451	quash	1	2484	re-displace	1	2517	replicate	1
2452	quench	1	2485	redouble	1	2518	repossess	1
2453	quieten	1	2486	redraw	1	2519	re-present	1
2454	quorate	1	2487	re-elect	1	2520	repulse	1
2455	race	1	2488	re-emit	1	2521	requisition	1
2456	radicalise	1	2489	re-engage	1	2522	re-read	1
2457	radio-label	1	2490	re-engrave	1	2523	rescind	1
2458	raid	1	2491	re-excavate	1	2524	resell	1
2459	rally	1	2492	re-explain	1	2525	re-size	1
2460	ram	1	2493	referee	1	2526	resorb	1
2461	ranch	1	2494	refill	1	2527	resort	1
2462	range-gate	1	2495	refortify	1	2528	respond	1
2463	ransack	1	2496	refresh	1	2529	restructure	1
2464	rather	1	2497	refrigerate	1	2530	retard	1
2465	ration	1	2498	refurnish	1	2531	re-think	1
2466	rawl bolt	1	2499	regale	1	2532	retie	1
2467	realign	1	2500	regurgitate	1	2533	retighten	1
2468	reanimate	1	2501	reheat	1	2534	retort	1
2469	reappoint	1	2502	rehouse	1	2535	retrace	1

2536	retract	1	2569	scotch	1	2602	slay	1
2537	retrain	1	2570	scramble	1	2603	sling	1
2538	retune	1	2571	scream	1	2604	slope	1
2539	return fold	1	2572	scribble	1	2605	slot	1
2540	reunite	1	2573	script	1	2606	smack	1
2541	revolutionise	1	2574	scrutinise	1	2607	smoke	1
2542	revolve	1	2575	seat	1	2608	snag	1
2543	rewire	1	2576	second-guess	1	2609	snare	1
2544	rim	1	2577	secularise	1	2610	sneeze	1
2545	rinse	1	2578	segment	1	2611	sniff	1
2546	ripen	1	2579	self-create	1	2612	snub	1
2547	rivet	1	2580	self-employ	1	2613	sock	1
2548	roam	1	2581	sensitise	1	2614	solicit	1
2549	rough	1	2582	serialise	1	2615	spark	1
2550	ruck	1	2583	shame	1	2616	spatter	1
2551	ruffle	1	2584	sheath	1	2617	speak/see	1
2552	rumble	1	2585	sheet	1	2618	spearhead	1
2553	rumour	1	2586	shelter	1	2619	spew	1
2554	rustle	1	2587	shepherd	1	2620	spirit	1
2555	safety-check	1	2588	shore	1	2621	splurt	1
2556	sail	1	2589	short circuit	1	2622	spoil	1
2557	salve	1	2590	shorten	1	2623	spoon	1
2558	sample	1	2591	shovel	1	2624	sprain	1
2559	sap	1	2592	shred	1	2625	spray-paint	1
2560	sauté	1	2593	shroud	1	2626	stagger	1
2561	savour	1	2594	shunt	1	2627	stalk	1
2562	scandalise	1	2595	side-foot	1	2628	stampede	1
2563	scar	1	2596	sideline	1	2629	stare	1
2564	scheme	1	2597	single	1	2630	startle	1
2565	school	1	2598	sip	1	2631	station	1
2566	scoff	1	2599	siphon	1	2632	stencil	1
2567	scorch	1	2600	size	1	2633	step	1
2568	scorn	1	2601	skirt	1	2634	stipulate	1

2635	stitch	1
2636	stoke	1
2637	stomp	1
2638	strangle	1
2639	streamline	1
2640	strum	1
2641	stump	1
2642	sub-develop	1
2643	subjugate	1
2644	sublet	1
2645	submerge	1
2646	subordinate	1
2647	substitute	1
2648	substract	1
2649	subtract	1
2650	suffix	1
2651	suffuse	1
2652	surpass	1
2653	swathe	1
2654	sway	1
2655	swish	1
2656	swivel	1
2657	synchronize	1
2658	syphon	1
2659	tag	1
2660	tailor	1
2661	taint	1
2662	tame	1
2663	tamper	1
2664	tarnish	1
2665	tattoo	1
2666	taunt	1
2667	tend	1

2668	testify	1
2669	theorise	1
2670	thin	1
2671	thrash	1
2672	thresh	1
2673	thwack	1
2674	tile	1
2675	till	1
2676	tinge	1
2677	tint	1
2678	tot	1
2679	tout	1
2680	track/gain	1
2681	transfer-list	1
2682	transmute	1
2683	transpire	1
2684	transplant	1
2685	trans-ship	1
2686	traverse	1
2687	triangulate	1
2688	trivialise	1
2689	troop	1
2690	trot	1
2691	tug	1
2692	typeset	1
2693	typify	1
2694	unbalance	1
2695	unblock	1
2696	unclip	1
2697	uncork	1
2698	undercut	1
2699	underrate	1
2700	underspecify	1

2701	understanding/ explaining	1
2702	underwork	1
2703	undisguise	1
2704	undisturb	1
2705	unemploy	1
2706	unhinge	1
2707	unholster	1
2708	unlock	1
2709	unmake	1
2710	unmask	1
2711	unprotect	1
2712	unroll	1
2713	unsettle	1
2714	untreat	1
2715	untrouble	1
2716	uproot	1
2717	upstage	1
2718	usurp	1
2719	vaccinate	1
2720	valley	1
2721	venerate	1
2722	ventilate	1
2723	venture	1
2724	verse	1
2725	veto	1
2726	video	1
2727	vindicate	1
2728	visualize	1
2729	vivify	1
2730	volatilize	1
2731	vulgarise	1
2732	wad	1

付　録

2733	waft	1
2734	wangle	1
2735	wean	1
2736	wed	1
2737	wedge	1
2738	whet	1
2739	whisk	1

2740	whisper	1
2741	wink	1
2742	winkle	1
2743	wire	1
2744	word	1
2745	word process	1
2746	worsen	1

2747	wrack	1
2748	wrest	1
2749	wrong-foot	1
2750	x-ray	1
2751	yearn	1
2752	zip	1

Dimonotransitive

1	tell	155
2	ask	60
3	remind	21
4	show	6
5	inform	5
6	advise	3
7	answer	2
8	assure	2

9	give	2
10	beckon	1
11	behove	1
12	call	1
13	convince	1
14	cost	1
15	offer	1
16	pay	1

17	promise	1
18	quote	1
19	send	1
20	strike	1
21	supply	1
22	take	1
23	warn	1
24	write	1

Ditransitive

1	give	560
2	tell	484
3	ask	91
4	show	82
5	send	78
6	offer	54
7	get	29
8	cost	23
9	teach	23
10	allow	20
11	convince	20
12	inform	20
13	pay	18
14	remind	16

15	assure	13
16	buy	12
17	do	12
18	lend	12
19	take	12
20	promise	11
21	warn	10
22	cause	9
23	grant	9
24	owe	9
25	wish	9
26	deny	8
27	earn	8
28	leave	8

29	persuade	8
30	award	7
31	bring	7
32	guarantee	7
33	advise	6
34	charge	5
35	hand	5
36	save	5
37	write	5
38	afford	4
39	allocate	4
40	assign	4
41	drop	4
42	accord	3

147

43	cook	3
44	make	3
45	refuse	3
46	satisfy	3
47	set	3
48	spare	3
49	cut	2
50	design	2
51	find	2
52	fine	2
53	lose	2
54	order	2
55	pass	2
56	play	2
57	quote	2

58	reassure	2
59	throw	2
60	win	2
61	bet	1
62	build	1
63	call	1
64	command	1
65	deal	1
66	deliver	1
67	direct	1
68	draw	1
69	feed	1
70	file	1
71	instruct	1
72	keep	1

73	loan	1
74	notify	1
75	overpay	1
76	permit	1
77	prescribe	1
78	profit	1
79	purchase	1
80	read	1
81	render	1
82	rent	1
83	sell	1
84	serve	1
85	supply	1
86	surprise	1
87	vote	1

Complex-transitive

1	make	500
2	call	480
3	put	390
4	get	236
5	keep	213
6	find	205
7	have	142
8	see	132
9	leave	112
10	take	109
11	describe	91
12	regard	82
13	bring	81
14	know	81
15	place	74
16	consider	49

17	set	49
18	use	44
19	turn	42
20	think	33
21	send	29
22	date	28
23	hold	28
24	bear	25
25	treat	24
26	name	20
27	term	20
28	play	19
29	define	18
30	drive	16
31	lay	16
32	push	15

33	render	15
34	show	14
35	carry	12
36	cut	12
37	force	12
38	recognize	12
39	stick	11
40	view	11
41	declare	10
42	mark	10
43	move	10
44	appoint	9
45	entitle	9
46	label	9
47	locate	9
48	map	9

付　録

49	build	8	82	contain	4	115	kick	3
50	like	8	83	deem	4	116	nickname	3
51	reduce	8	84	deposit	4	117	offer	3
52	accept	7	85	dismiss	4	118	pack	3
53	base	7	86	maintain	4	119	position	3
54	cast	7	87	pass	4	120	prove	3
55	categorize	7	88	pin	4	121	represent	3
56	include	7	89	plant	4	122	shape	3
57	let	7	90	pour	4	123	shoot	3
58	pull	7	91	present	4	124	strip	3
59	throw	7	92	refer	4	125	tip	3
60	allow	6	93	register	4	126	train	3
61	catch	6	94	rule	4	127	acknowledge	2
62	feel	6	95	strike	4	128	adjudge	2
63	fit	6	96	want	4	129	adopt	2
64	knock	6	97	bung	3	130	blow	2
65	lead	6	98	claim	3	131	channel	2
66	lock	6	99	class	3	132	choose	2
67	paint	6	100	conceive	3	133	cite	2
68	perceive	6	101	confine	3	134	clamp	2
69	situate	6	102	denounce	3	135	commit	2
70	convert	5	103	display	3	136	consign	2
71	interpret	5	104	divide	3	137	construct	2
72	portray	5	105	drop	3	138	deliver	2
73	shove	5	106	elect	3	139	depict	2
74	sit	5	107	establish	3	140	designate	2
75	transform	5	108	give	3	141	diagnose	2
76	tuck	5	109	hail	3	142	draw	2
77	wrap	5	110	head	3	143	dub	2
78	write	5	111	house	3	144	dump	2
79	believe	4	112	identify	3	145	engrave	2
80	bury	4	113	intend	3	146	enter	2
81	code name	4	114	invite	3	147	fix	2

148	fold	2
149	hammer	2
150	hear	2
151	help	2
152	hide	2
153	imagine	2
154	impose	2
155	incorporate	2
156	insert	2
157	introduce	2
158	judge	2
159	land	2
160	lever	2
161	lift	2
162	list	2
163	live	2
164	load	2
165	mount	2
166	nail	2
167	need	2
168	open	2
169	park	2
170	pile	2
171	prise	2
172	proclaim	2
173	provide	2
174	punch	2
175	rate	2
176	read	2
177	remember	2
178	roll	2
179	run	2
180	say	2

181	serve	2
182	slap	2
183	slip	2
184	sprinkle	2
185	suggest	2
186	superimpose	2
187	tie	2
188	transfer	2
189	value	2
190	wash	2
191	wear	2
192	welcome	2
193	absorb	1
194	add	1
195	address	1
196	advert	1
197	agree	1
198	anchor	1
199	apply	1
200	arrange	1
201	ask	1
202	assign	1
203	attack	1
204	blend	1
205	book	1
206	bounce	1
207	brand	1
208	break	1
209	brush	1
210	bundle	1
211	burn	1
212	catapult	1
213	centre	1

214	characterise	1
215	chip	1
216	chop	1
217	chuck	1
218	circulate	1
219	classify	1
220	clear	1
221	clip	1
222	comb	1
223	combine	1
224	compare	1
225	concern	1
226	construe	1
227	count	1
228	cover	1
229	create	1
230	credit	1
231	develop	1
232	devote	1
233	dice	1
234	discover	1
235	divert	1
236	draft	1
237	drag	1
238	edge	1
239	edit	1
240	embed	1
241	encapsulate	1
242	enhance	1
243	entice	1
244	erode	1
245	express	1
246	fancy	1

247	fashion	1	280	notice	1	313	report	1
248	feed	1	281	number	1	314	reverse	1
249	ferry	1	282	observe	1	315	riddle	1
250	flick	1	283	order	1	316	rout	1
251	forecast	1	284	package	1	317	sandwich	1
252	form	1	285	pay	1	318	scale	1
253	funnel	1	286	persuade	1	319	scoop	1
254	gloss	1	287	plaster	1	320	score	1
255	glue	1	288	plug	1	321	segment	1
256	go	1	289	point	1	322	sell	1
257	group	1	290	pop	1	323	separate	1
258	haul	1	291	post	1	324	settle	1
259	hit	1	292	praise	1	325	shake	1
260	hoist	1	293	prepare	1	326	shrink	1
261	hurl	1	294	prescribe	1	327	site	1
262	import	1	295	preserve	1	328	slide	1
263	incarcerate	1	296	press	1	329	slot	1
264	influence	1	297	presume	1	330	smooth	1
265	inject	1	298	price	1	331	spill	1
266	install	1	299	project	1	332	split	1
267	jerk	1	300	promote	1	333	spool	1
268	lean	1	301	propose	1	334	spot	1
269	link	1	302	publish	1	335	squeeze	1
270	lob	1	303	pump	1	336	squirt	1
271	lose	1	304	quarter	1	337	stamp	1
272	lure	1	305	raise	1	338	stash	1
273	march	1	306	rank	1	339	station	1
274	measure	1	307	receive	1	340	stir	1
275	misread	1	308	reconvert	1	341	stream	1
276	mix	1	309	re-elect	1	342	stroke	1
277	modify	1	310	regroup	1	343	stuff	1
278	nestle	1	311	re-model	1	344	suck	1
279	nip	1	312	rename	1	345	support	1

346	swallow	1
347	symbolize	1
348	tell	1
349	thread	1
350	thrust	1
351	tickle	1
352	tout	1
353	trace	1
354	translate	1

355	transmute	1
356	transpose	1
357	trap	1
358	unite	1
359	upgrade	1
360	visualize	1
361	vote	1
362	wave	1
363	weigh	1

364	wheel	1
365	whip	1
366	whiz	1
367	win	1
368	wish	1
369	worry	1
370	wrench	1
371	wrestle	1

Transitive

1	allow	217
2	let	192
3	have	179
4	see	170
5	make	151
6	get	142
7	want	134
8	ask	115
9	expect	97
10	enable	89
11	find	64
12	hear	61
13	help	61
14	encourage	58
15	force	50
16	cause	40
17	require	37
18	think	34
19	stop	31
20	say	29
21	like	27
22	show	27

23	keep	26
24	tell	26
25	invite	25
26	consider	24
27	urge	24
28	leave	23
29	advise	21
30	feel	21
31	believe	19
32	lead	19
33	tempt	19
34	watch	19
35	entitle	17
36	persuade	17
37	remember	17
38	intend	16
39	prevent	16
40	imagine	14
41	know	13
42	oblige	13
43	mean	11
44	permit	11

45	take	11
46	order	9
47	empower	8
48	need	8
49	set	8
50	warn	8
51	bring	7
52	teach	7
53	assume	6
54	hold	6
55	send	6
56	commission	5
57	compel	5
58	deem	5
59	design	5
60	prefer	5
61	report	5
62	train	5
63	instruct	4
64	mind	4
65	save	4
66	understand	4

67	wish	4
68	appoint	3
69	choose	3
70	condition	3
71	discover	3
72	drive	3
73	employ	3
74	estimate	3
75	involve	3
76	perceive	3
77	plan	3
78	project	3
79	prompt	3
80	reckon	3
81	recommend	3
82	schedule	3
83	acknowledge	2
84	activate	2
85	assist	2
86	attract	2
87	catch	2
88	detect	2
89	equip	2
90	guarantee	2
91	induce	2
92	influence	2
93	inspire	2
94	notice	2
95	observe	2
96	prepare	2
97	propose	2
98	qualify	2

99	start	2
100	trust	2
101	accept	1
102	aid	1
103	aim	1
104	allege	1
105	appreciate	1
106	avoid	1
107	behold	1
108	calculate	1
109	call	1
110	certify	1
111	challenge	1
112	command	1
113	condemn	1
114	confirm	1
115	convince	1
116	cover	1
117	delay	1
118	designate	1
119	destine	1
120	determine	1
121	direct	1
122	educate	1
123	encounter	1
124	enjoin	1
125	fancy	1
126	forbid	1
127	forgive	1
128	glimpse	1
129	impell	1
130	implore	1

131	judge	1
132	liken	1
133	mention	1
134	necessitate	1
135	nominate	1
136	overhear	1
137	position	1
138	possess	1
139	predispose	1
140	press	1
141	proclaim	1
142	program	1
143	read	1
144	realize	1
145	recognize	1
146	regard	1
147	remind	1
148	represent	1
149	request	1
150	retain	1
151	select	1
152	sense	1
153	state	1
154	stir	1
155	summon	1
156	suppose	1
157	switch	1
158	task	1
159	term	1
160	veto	1
161	visualize	1
162	will	1

付録2．中学校学習指導要領の必修語として共通する動詞

1	answer	21	forget	41	make	61	speak
2	arrive	22	get	42	meet	62	stand
3	ask	23	give	43	need	63	stop
4	be	24	go	44	open	64	study
5	become	25	grow	45	play	65	swim
6	begin	26	have	46	please	66	take
7	bring	27	hear	47	put	67	talk
8	build	28	help	48	read	68	teach
9	buy	29	hope	49	ride	69	tell
10	call	30	invite	50	rise	70	thank
11	carry	31	keep	51	run	71	think
12	catch	32	know	52	say	72	try
13	come	33	learn	53	see	73	understand
14	cry	34	leave	54	sell	74	use
15	cut	35	lend	55	send	75	visit
16	drink	36	let	56	show	76	walk
17	eat	37	like	57	sing	77	want
18	find	38	listen	58	sit	78	wash
19	finish	39	live	59	sleep	79	work
20	fly	40	look	60	smile	80	write

付録3. Fries and Fries（1961）の動詞

1	be	33	collect	65	visit	97	expect
2	ask	34	come	66	walk	98	explain
3	begin	35	cover	67	want (to)	99	fasten
4	close	36	cut	68	wash	100	feel
5	count	37	divide	69	work	101	fly
6	do	38	erase	70	add	102	forget
7	give	39	fall	71	admit	103	freeze
8	have	40	find	72	afford	104	grow
9	hold	41	get	73	agree	105	happen (to)
10	know	42	go	74	arrive	106	harvest
11	like	43	hear	75	become	107	help
12	look	44	heat	76	believe	108	hire
13	make	45	learn	77	borrow	109	include
14	name	46	listen	78	break	110	increase
15	number	47	live	79	buy	111	intend
16	open	48	meet	80	carry	112	interrupt
17	put	49	move	81	catch	113	invite
18	repeat	50	own	82	change	114	join
19	see	51	play	83	chase	115	keep
20	show	52	point	84	choose	116	kill
21	sit	53	raise	85	consider	117	kiss
22	take (out)	54	read	86	cost	118	lay
23	tell	55	remember	87	cross	119	leave
24	thank	56	send	88	cultivate	120	lend
25	understand	57	sleep	89	decrease	121	let
26	watch	58	speak	90	decide	122	lie
27	write	59	stand	91	deliver	123	marry
28	build	60	stay	92	drink	124	mean
29	burn	61	strike	93	drive	125	mention
30	call	62	study	94	dig	126	mind
31	celebrate	63	swim	95	earn	127	need
32	clean	64	use	96	excuse	128	note

129	order
130	pay
131	pick
132	plant
133	plow
134	present
135	promise
136	reach
137	receive
138	rent

139	rest
140	ride
141	ripen
142	rise
143	roast
144	run
145	say
146	seem
147	sell
148	separate

149	set
150	sign
151	sing
152	slice
153	smile
154	talk
155	teach
156	think
157	throw
158	toss

159	try
160	turn
161	wade
162	wait
163	wake
164	wish
165	wonder
166	worry

付録4．LDOCEの定義語内の動詞

1	accept	33	break	65	cut	97	express
2	achieve	34	bring	66	decide	98	face
3	act	35	build	67	deliver	99	fall
4	add	36	buy	68	depend	100	feed
5	admit	37	call	69	describe	101	feel
6	advise	38	care	70	design	102	fight
7	affect	39	carry	71	destroy	103	fill
8	afford	40	catch	72	develop	104	find
9	agree	41	cause	73	die	105	finish
10	aim	42	change	74	direct	106	fit
11	allow	43	charge	75	discover	107	fix
12	announce	44	check	76	discuss	108	fly
13	answer	45	choose	77	divide	109	follow
14	appear	46	claim	78	do	110	force
15	approve	47	clean	79	draw	111	forget
16	argue	48	clear	80	dress	112	form
17	arrange	49	close	81	drink	113	gain
18	arrive	50	collect	82	drive	114	gather
19	ask	51	come	83	drop	115	get
20	attach	52	commit	84	earn	116	give
21	attack	53	compare	85	eat	117	go
22	attend	54	complete	86	emphasize	118	grow
23	attract	55	connect	87	employ	119	guess
24	avoid	56	consider	88	encourage	120	handle
25	base	57	contain	89	end	121	hang
26	be	58	continue	90	enjoy	122	happen
27	bear	59	control	91	enter	123	hate
28	beat	60	cost	92	establish	124	have
29	become	61	count	93	exist	125	hear
30	begin	62	cover	94	expect	126	help
31	believe	63	cross	95	experience	127	hide
32	belong	64	cry	96	explain	128	hit

129	hold	162	match	195	provide	228	sell
130	hope	163	matter	196	pull	229	send
131	ignore	164	mean	197	push	230	separate
132	imagine	165	measure	198	put	231	serve
133	improve	166	meet	199	raise	232	set
134	include	167	mention	200	reach	233	settle
135	increase	168	mind	201	read	234	share
136	influence	169	miss	202	realize	235	shoot
137	intend	170	move	203	receive	236	shout
138	introduce	171	name	204	recognize	237	show
139	invite	172	need	205	reduce	238	shut
140	involve	173	notice	206	refer	239	sing
141	join	174	obtain	207	refuse	240	sit
142	keep	175	offer	208	regard	241	sleep
143	kill	176	open	209	remain	242	slow
144	knock	177	order	210	remember	243	smile
145	know	178	organize	211	remind	244	smoke
146	laugh	179	own	212	remove	245	sound
147	lead	180	pass	213	repeat	246	speak
148	learn	181	pay	214	replace	247	spend
149	leave	182	persuade	215	report	248	spread
150	let	183	pick	216	represent	249	stamp
151	lie	184	place	217	return	250	stand
152	lift	185	plan	218	ride	251	start
153	like	186	play	219	ring	252	stay
154	listen	187	prefer	220	rise	253	stop
155	live	188	prepare	221	roll	254	suffer
156	look	189	press	222	run	255	suggest
157	lose	190	prevent	223	satisfy	256	support
158	love	191	produce	224	save	257	suppose
159	make	192	promise	225	say	258	take
160	manage	193	protect	226	see	259	talk
161	marry	194	prove	227	seem	260	teach

261	tell
262	tend
263	thank
264	think
265	threaten
266	throw
267	touch

268	train
269	travel
270	treat
271	try
272	turn
273	understand
274	use

275	visit
276	wait
277	walk
278	want
279	wash
280	watch
281	wear

282	win
283	wish
284	work
285	worry
286	write

英語索引

A

activity / activity verbs / Activity verbs　58, 59, 60, 65, 66, 67, 79, 80, 81
antonymy　6
aspectual / aspectual verbs / Aspectual verbs　58, 63, 66, 67, 79, 81
associations　4, 6, 10, 14, 15
auditory input lexicon　12, 13
auxiliary verb　58

B

Basic English　vi, 21, 22, 23
　　　Basic English System　23
British National Corpus (BNC)　26, 58
　　BNC　58
The British component of the International Corpus of English　vi, 7, 33
　　ICE-GB　33, 34, 36, 37, 40, 42, 45, 46, 57, 58, 68, 74, 77, 78, 79, 82, 83, 85, 87, 88, 92
　　ICE grammar　37
Bullon, Stephen　28

C

Carter　14, 15, 16
causative / causative verbs / Causative verbs　58, 61, 66, 79, 80
clause type　vi, 7, 14, 73, 74, 76, 77, 78, 79, 80, 82, 85, 87, 92
collocational patterns　15
collocations　4, 6, 10, 13, 14, 15
communication / communication verbs / Communication verbs　58, 60, 65, 66, 79, 80
complementation pattern　36, 37

complex transitive / complex-transitive / complex transitive verbs / complex-transitive verbs   7, 37, 39, 64, 65, 77, 90
components of the meaning   18
components theory   18
concept and referents   4, 5, 7, 10, 14, 15
constraints on use   4, 6, 12, 14, 15
Cook   16, 17, 19
copular / Copular / copular verbs / Copular verbs   7, 37, 38, 46, 56, 64, 65, 77, 89

D

dimonotransitive / dimonotransitive verbs   7, 37, 38, 77, 90
ditransitive / ditransitive verbs   7, 37, 39, 64, 77, 90
ditto   46

E

-ed participle   37
Ellis   12, 13, 14, 15
entailment   6
ESP（English for Specific Purposes）   91
existence / Existence verbs   66, 67, 79, 81
    verbs of existence or relationship   58, 62

F

feature / features   36, 37, 42
Form   3, 4, 7, 13, 15
form and meaning   4, 7, 14, 15
frequency   4, 12, 24
Fries and Fries   68-69, 70, 71, 87, 88, 92
Fuzzy Tree Fragment   46

G

general English   23

A General Service List of English Words　vi, 23
　　GSL, the *GSL*　21, 23, 24, 91
　　The General Service List　24
Graded Readers　vi, 21, 30
grammatical class　13
grammatical functions　4, 6, 10, 14, 15
Grammaticon　40, 46, 57
　　Grammaticon Options　40

H

headword / headwords　24
homonym / Homonyms　5, 27
hyponymy　6

I

infinitive　37
-ing participle　37
intransitive / intransitive verbs　7, 37, 45, 64, 65, 77, 78, 88

J

JACET 8000　21, 26, 27, 28, 30, 85
　　JACET 8000 plus 250　27

L

lexical specifications　13
lexical verbs　36, 58, 64
lexicon / Lexicon　41, 45, 46, 56, 67
　　Lexicon Options　41, 42
The Longman Defining Vocabulary　21, 28, 31
Longman Dictionary of Contemporary English（1977）　68
Longman Dictionary of Contemporary English（2003）　7
　　LDOCE　7, 16, 28, 29, 30, 31, 68, 69, 70, 71, 86, 87, 88, 92
Longman Grammar of Spoken and Written English（1999）　vi, 33, 58

LGSWE 58, 64, 65, 68, 70, 74, 75, 80, 81, 83, 87, 88, 92
Longman Lexicon of Contemporary English（1981） vi, 33, 67
    LLCE 67, 68

M

main verb 58
mapping of word form 13
Meaning 4, 5, 7, 14, 15
meaning representations 13
mental / mental verbs / Mental verbs 58, 60, 65, 66, 79, 80, 81
meronymy 6
Miller and Fellbaum 6
monotransitive / Monotransitive / monotransitive verbs / Monotransitive verbs
    7, 37, 38, 64, 77, 78, 79, 83, 89
multi-word unit 46

N

Nagy 5
Nation 3, 7, 13, 14, 15, 27
Nation and Waring 24
New FTF 46, 47
node（節点） 34
    node / Node 40, 42, 46

O

occurrence / Occurrence verbs 66, 79, 81
    verbs of simple occurrence 58, 62
Ogden, C.K. 21
OPERATIONS 21, 22

P

parts of speech 24
pragmatic and discoursal functions 15

primary verbs　58, 64
productive knowledge　4
prototype theory　18

Q, R

QUALITIES　21, 22
range　24
recall　14
receptive knowledge　4
reference specification　5
register　4, 12
relative coreness　15
Richards　22

S

semantic and conceptual properties　13
semantic fields　→意味領域（semantic fields）を参照
　　Arts and Crafts, Science and Technology, Industry and Education　67, 70
　　The Body: its Functions and Welfare　67, 70, 71
　　Buildings, Houses, the Home, Clothes, Belongings, and Personal Care
　　　67, 70
　　Entertainment, Sports, and Games　67, 70
　　Feelings, Emotions, Attitudes, and Sensations　67, 70, 71
　　Food, Drink, and Farming　67, 70, 71
　　General and Abstract Terms　68, 70, 71
　　Life and living Things　67, 68, 70
　　Movement, Location, Travel, and Transport　67-68, 70, 71
　　Numbers, Measurement, Money, and Commerce　67, 70
　　People and the Family　67, 70
　　Space and Time　67, 70
　　Substances, Materials, Objects, and Equipment　67, 70, 71
　　Thought and Communication, Language and Grammar　67, 70, 71
sense selection　5

sequence information   13
speech output lexicon   12, 13
spelling output lexicon   12, 13
spoken form   4, 13, 15, 17
SUMMARY OF RULES   21, 22
Summers, Della   28
Summers et al.   28
synonymy   6
syntactic frames   14

T

thesaurus-dictionary   67
THINGS   21, 22
TOEFL   26, 27
TOEIC   26, 27
transitive / Transitive   7, 37, 65, 77, 90
transitivity   37, 39, 42, 45, 46, 54, 56, 57, 58, 90
troponymy   6

U, V

Use   4, 6, 10, 14, 15
visual input lexicon   12, 13

W

West / West, Michael   23, 24, 91
word form   5
word parts   4, 7, 14, 15
written corpus   24
written form   4, 13, 15, 17

… 日 本 語 索 引

あ

アウトプット　12, 13
暗唱　16
安藤他　21

い

異形　45, 54, 74, 75, 79
異語　91
　　異語数　57, 58
イディオム　16
意味　3, 4, 5, 18, 19, 27
意味的特性　12, 14
意味領域（semantic domain）　58, 73, 74
　　意味領域　58, 64, 65, 66, 67, 75, 79, 80, 81, 82, 83
意味領域（semantic fields）　67
　　意味領域　68, 69, 70, 71
　　意味の領域　69
「入り口の語彙」　31
インプット　12, 13

う, え

馬本　31
英語構造　v
　　英語の基本構造　v, 19, 72, 85, 87, 92
　　英語の構造　v, 85, 92
英語母語話者　v, vi, 12, 13, 19, 68, 82, 83, 85, 86, 92
SVAパタン　65
SVOdAパタン　65
SVOdPoパタン　65
SVOdパタン　64
SVOiOdパタン　64
SVPsパタン　65
SVパタン　64

お, か

音形　19
概念と指示物　3, 18
下位範疇　41, 60
書き言葉　3, 18, 19, 30, 33, 58, 86, 87
　　書き言葉のコーパス　58
　　書き言葉のテクスト　36
学習解除　23
形　3, 16, 18
含意関係（entailment）　18

き, け

機能語　v, 6, 18, 73, 91
基本形　15, 74, 75, 79
基本動詞　vi, 71, 86, 87, 88, 93
　　基本動詞リスト　67, 85, 86
教育語彙　87
教育的観点　26
原形　45, 46, 54, 56, 74
言語活動　25, 26

言語材料　25, 26, 85, 91, 92

こ

コア　7
　コア性　93
　コアネス　15
語彙　v, vi, 16, 21, 22, 30, 31, 73, 82, 85, 91
　語彙学習　v
　語彙構造　12
　語彙項目　45, 56
　語彙習得　13
　語彙選定　vi, 72, 82
　語彙知識　3, 14
　学習語彙リスト　22
　語彙リスト　v, vi, 23, 25, 26, 27, 28, 30, 30-31にかかっている, 73, 85, 86, 87, 91, 92, 93
　語彙力　3
項構造（argument structure）　17, 18
　項構造　19
合成語　22
構成要素　28, 56
構文解析　58
コーパス　23, 26, 33, 40, 41, 59, 69, 85, 91, 92
語幹　4, 18
互換性　85
語義　vi, 3, 6, 23, 24, 30, 87, 92
語形　3, 5, 17, 18, 19, 21, 23, 24, 27, 36, 45, 58, 71, 72, 85
　語形の出現頻度　vi, 72, 91
語の集合（lexicon）　12

語形を中心とする頻度　85, 86
語源　5, 24, 27
語の位置　12
語の構成要素　3, 18
コミュニケーション活動　60
コミュニケーションの受容　60
コロケーション　3, 15, 17, 18
語を「知っている」　v, 3, 5, 14, 15, 17, 18, 19

さ, し

サイズ　6, 18
指示的特性　12
自動詞　67
JACET 8000サブコーパス　26
出現頻度　7, 19, 23, 28, 30, 45, 46, 54, 82, 86, 87
出現頻度順　16
受容語彙　3, 26, 30, 72
主要動詞　39
上位・下位関係（troponymy）　18
使用域　19, 64, 86
使用頻度　v, 29

せ

生活語彙　25
接辞　4, 18, 21
節点　→node（節点）を参照
全体・部分語関係（meronymy）　18

た, ち

大学英語教育学会基本語リスト　vi, 26

タイプ　6, 18
多義　16, 93
多義性　5
竹蓋・中條　vi, 21, 25, 26, 30, 85
他動詞　39, 67
田中他（2003）　7
中学校学習指導要領　v, 73
　　学習指導要領　v, vi, 7, 68, 70, 71, 73, 74, 75, 76, 77, 78, 79, 80, 81, 82, 83, 86, 87, 91, 92

て

定義　7, 28, 31
定義可能度　31
定義語　28, 29, 30, 31, 68, 69, 86, 92
定義動詞　87
dittoタグ　46, 47
dittoタグ付きの動詞　46, 47, 48, 54, 56, 57
テクスト　41
　　テクスト・ユニット（文）　58
　　テクストカテゴリー　34
　　テクストコード　34, 37
「出口を意識した語彙」　31
出口側のリスト　30

と

同意関係（synonymy）　18
同形語　27
統合価パタン（valency pattern）　58
　　統合価パタン　64, 65, 66, 67
統語構造　15
統語的特性　12

動詞　6, 7, 17, 18, 19, 21, 22, 23, 24, 27, 29, 30, 33, 37, 39, 40, 41, 42, 46, 54, 56, 57, 58, 59, 60, 61, 62, 63, 64, 65, 66, 67, 68, 69, 70, 71, 72, 74, 75, 76, 77, 78, 80, 81, 82, 83, 86, 87, 91, 92
　　動詞句　17
　　動詞の型　85
　　動詞のパタン　68, 69
　　動詞のリスト　45, 46
　　動詞の割合　75, 76, 81, 86, 87

な, に

内容語　6, 18
日本人英語初学者　v, vi, 3, 12, 19, 25, 31, 67, 68, 74, 82, 85, 86, 87, 88, 91, 92

は

発表語彙　3
話し言葉　3, 18, 19, 33, 86, 87
　　話し言葉のコーパス　58
　　話し言葉のテクスト　36
反意関係（antonymy）　18
反意語　22
範疇　58
伴立（命題と結論の関係）　12

ひ

必修語　vi, 7, 73, 75, 76, 81, 82, 91
必要最低限の語彙　v
非定形節　39
品詞　6, 18, 23, 24, 27, 28, 30, 40, 46, 74

品詞のタグ付け　33
　　　品詞のラベル付け　28, 29, 30, 86
頻度　21, 27, 28, 31, 85, 86

　　　　　　ふ，ほ
不規則変化　17, 18
複合語　16, 27, 28
文構造　17
文法シラバス　91
文法的機能　3, 18
文法的タグ付き　92
文法的な分析　33
文法的範疇（品詞）　17
文法パタン　6, 14, 18
包摂関係（hyponymy）　18

　　　　　　み，め，も
見出し語　23, 27, 29, 30, 31, 68, 86
メンタルレキシコン　6, 12

目標領域における語彙　vi

　　　　　　ゆ，よ
有効度　25, 26, 27
用法　3, 18, 27, 30, 58
用法における制約　3, 19

　　　　　　る，れ，ろ
類義語　7, 68, 93
類義性　92
歴史的語彙リスト　vi, 21, 30
連結動詞　62, 63
連語　6, 18, 27
連想　3, 18
論題（Arguments）　71

　　　　　　わ
ワード・ファミリー　4, 18

著者略歴

土岸 真由美（どぎし まゆみ）

1979年　広島県に生まれる
2001年　安田女子大学文学部英語英米文学科 卒業
　　　　安田女子大学大学院文学研究科英語学英米文学専攻博士前期課程 入学
2003年　安田女子大学大学院文学研究科英語学英米文学専攻博士前期課程 修了
　　　　安田女子大学大学院文学研究科英語学英米文学専攻博士後期課程 入学
2009年　安田女子大学大学院文学研究科英語学英米文学専攻博士後期課程 修了

学　　位　博士（文学）

現　　職　広島修道大学「e-learning英語」担当契約教員（講師）

主要論文　「中学校における必修語─動詞(3)─：意味のコア性の観点から」『中国地区英語教育学会研究紀要』35, 2005年（中国地区英語教育学会誌），"In Search of Basic Verbs for Japanese Learners of EFL at the Junior High School Level: A View from 'Coreness'" *Annual Review of English Language Education in Japan, 17*, 2006（全国英語教育学会誌），「eラーニングを活用した英語授業の実践報告」『安田女子大学大学院文学研究科紀要』15, 2010年　ほか

日本人英語初学者のための基本動詞選定に関する研究

　　　　　　　　　　　　　　　　　　　平成23年4月11日　発　行

　　　著　者　土岸　真由美
　　　発行所　㈱溪水社
　　　　　　　広島市中区小町1-4（〒730-0041）
　　　　　　　電話（082）246-7909／FAX（082）246-7876
　　　　　　　e-mail: info@keisui.co.jp

ISBN978-4-86327-133-3 C3082